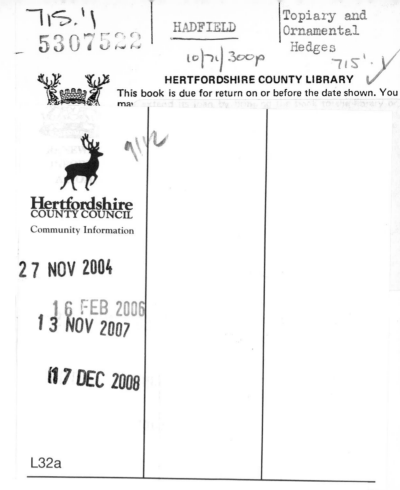
Please renew/return this item by the last date shown.

So that your telephone call is charged at local rate,
please call the numbers as set out below:

	From Area codes 01923 or 0208:	From the rest of Herts:
Renewals:	01923 471373	01438 737373
Enquiries:	01923 471333	01438 737333
Minicom:	01923 471599	01438 737599

L32b

TOPIARY

AND

ORNAMENTAL HEDGES

Drummond Castle today (page 50)

Miles Hadfield

TOPIARY
AND
ORNAMENTAL HEDGES

THEIR HISTORY AND CULTIVATION

ADAM & CHARLES BLACK
LONDON

FIRST PUBLISHED 1971
BY A. & C. BLACK LIMITED
4, 5 & 6 SOHO SQUARE LONDON WIV 6AD

© MILES HADFIELD 1971

ISBN 7136 1193 6

Printed in Great Britain by
W & J Mackay & Co Ltd, Chatham, Kent

Contents

Illustrations

Introduction

The craft, or occasionally art, of gardening (as distinct from horticulture, the mere cultivation of plants) can be divided into two kinds. The first is that which violently defies nature to show man's domination of it—as, for example, by ejecting water high in the sky from the nozzle of a fountain. In the second, the gardener soothes the water and conjures it to flow calmly along serpentine paths. The first predominated from ancient times until, perhaps, the early eighteenth century, when a handful of Englishmen, confident in man's innate superiority over the natural world, decided to accept it as an ally with whom he could play.

On this latter point the world has subsequently been divided, the English for the most part dominant in holding the latter view, even giving the movement the international name of *le jardin anglais*. Elsewhere, and from time to time even in the British Isles itself, those who would impose formality on the natural scene have usually triumphed: the philosophy of the architect who is concerned with spaces, forms and surfaces conceived by man is followed.

Thus rather pompously and crudely one may define the two fundamental opposing philosophies of gardening when these are carried out, however consciously, and their consequential styles.

Besides the management of water, the use of shears to modify the shapes of trees and shrubs is a touchstone of the two. This may take at least three forms— clipping them into forms which are purely abstract and architectural, clipping into forms which are extravagant, even comic, so as to catch the eye and divert the attention, and thirdly, the making of hedges which are more consequential than a barrier and play their part in a design. All these are vertical components in a design, used for example sometimes as an exclamation mark, at others as a row of columns.

There is, or perhaps it is now better to say was, another use of small and severely clipped shrubs—as a frame for the carpet-like patterns of parterres, spread flat over the ground.

These and their uses, and the cases for and against them—often fought quite fiercely—are an important part of the history of gardening and so a major item in the history of taste, British in particular. No doubt those now rather discredited and contradictory but still vociferous persons, the professional psychologists, could add even more to the discussion.

Closely allied to topiary is the use of hedges as part of a design for the forming of enclosures and making of divisions of a not entirely utilitarian purpose, as are the field hedges.

These, then, are the subjects discussed in this book, both from the often entertaining historical and the practical points of view.

I had intended adding a list of gardens open to the public with good examples illustrating this book. But the present rate of change would make it inaccurate in a year or two. I would recommend *The Shell Gardens Book*, edited by Peter Hunt, which includes a number of useful pictures which are valuable additions to those used here.

I am grateful to my brother John, from whose addiction to hedges and topiary over many years I have learned much. Miss Sandra Raphael has kindly supplied me with bibliographical and other information, Mr David Green has allowed me to make use of Henry Wise's planting lists in his *Gardener to Queen Anne*, and Mr Peter Hunt and Mr T. W. Jones have provided photographs, for all of which I am grateful, as well as to the Bodleian library for providing an illustration from *Hypnerotomatica Polyphili*.

CHAPTER 1

Origins

CYPRESS AND BOX

The earliest references to topiary seem to connect it with the Mediterranean cypress (*Cupressus sempervirens*). The fullest early account of this tree that I know is in the *Historia Naturalis* of Pliny the elder, one of the greatest observers and collectors of information in Roman times. He was born in AD 23 and lost his life in pursuit of his vocation when suffocated by the fumes of the eruption of Vesuvius which he was observing a little too closely at the time it spilled its lava over Pompeii and Herculaneum, 23rd August 79.

He tells us that the tree is an exotic (that is, it was not found as a native in Rome) and very difficult to rear, which was attested by the fact that M. Porcius Cato (234–149 BC), author of *De Re Rustica*, wrote about it at greater length than all the other trees. He pointed out that it is stubborn to grow, of no use for fruit, the foliage has a pungent smell, not even its shade is agreeable and its timber is scanty so that it almost belongs to the class of shrubs. It is consecrated to Dis, and consequently placed at the doors of houses as a sign of mourning. The female bears seed.

For a long time past, Pliny continues, owing to its pyramidal shape it was "not rejected" just for the purpose of marking the rows in vineyards, but nowadays it is clipped and made into thick walls or evenly rounded off with trim slenderness, and it is even made to provide the representations of the landscape gardener's work (*in picturas operi topiarii*) displaying hunting scenes, fleets of ships and imitations of real objects. There are two kinds of cypress, the female pyramidal tapering upwards, and the male which spreads its branches.

With present-day knowledge, it is interesting to comment on Pliny's observations. He was quite correct in his statement that the cypress was not a native of Italy. It is believed to be an indigenous tree, according to Augustine Henry, only in "the mountains of northern Persia, in Syria, Cilicia, Greece, and the islands of Rhodes, Crete and Cyprus". It has been carried by man to many parts of the world, and has even been planted in China. In many places it has long been naturalized. Cato's remarks that it was stubborn to grow are perplexing: it is easily raised from seed in a suitable climate, or under glass in a cool one.

The timber is still little if at all used, though it is supposed to have had certain uses in the past such as for the large chests used for importing silk for the Levant, as in Shakespeare's *Taming of the Shrew*:

> *In ivory coffers I have stuffed my crowns;*
> *In cypress chests my arras counterpoints,*
> *Costly apparel, tents and canopies.*

However, the name cypress has in the vernacular long been applied to many kinds of tree not belonging to the botanist's genus *Cupressus*—which is taken from the classical name of the tree.

The "male" and "female" trees no doubt refers to the two distinctive varieties of the tree found in nature. *Cupressus sempervirens stricta* is of narrow, flame-like shape. It is the "Italian" cypress of art and literature, and the type almost invariably cultivated on account of its beautiful form. It is the tree seen so often in paintings of the Italian scene; the "closed umbrella" opposed to the contrasting round-headed "open umbrella" or stone-pine (*Pinus pinea*) anciently associated with Roman religious procedure. The other variety, usually only found growing wild, is *C. s. horizontalis*, cedar-like with spreading branches.

It is strange that the Monterey cypress (*C. macrocarpa*), today lingering on as a wild tree only in a very limited part of the Monterey region of California, has two similar forms.

Finally, we come to Pliny's observation that the shaping of the tree was an example of the work of the landscape gardener—whom we can assume to be the garden designer—the *toparius*. It is remarkable that the name of a man with presumably so wide a range of activities should have been singled out and attached to but one of them, suggesting the importance of topiary in the later Roman gardens.

The association with the god Dis and mourning brings out one point. Herrick in his *Hesperides* (1648) wrote:

> To the Yew and Cypresse to grace his Funerall
> > *Both you two have*
> *Relations to the grave:*
> > *And where*
> The Fun'rall-Trump *sounds, you are there.*

On referring to the yew in Pliny, we find no such connection, nor does he refer to its use for topiary. Columella, writing at about the same time, regards it as little more than a weed.

The best-known account of the use of topiary in a Roman garden occurs in the letters of Pliny's nephew, Pliny the Younger (AD 62–110), in a description of his villa in Tuscany. He refers to a sort of terrace in front of the portico, "embellished with various figures and bounded with a box hedge, from whence you descend by an easy slope, adorned with the representation of divers animals in box, answering alternately to each other, into a lawn . . . this is surrounded by a walk enclosed with tonsile evergreens shaped into a variety of forms. Beyond it is the gestatio, laid out in the form of a circus, ornamented in the middle with box cut in numberless different figures, together with a plantation of shrubs, prevented by shears from shooting up too high."

Here we have an early example of an ornamental hedge. In another place, "box is cut into a thousand different forms: sometimes into letters expressing the name of the master; sometimes that of the artificer; whilst here and there little obelisks rise, intermixed with fruit trees".

Box is by now included on a liberal scale as a subject for Roman topiary.

The recent unearthing of the highly developed state of garden design and horticulture at Fishbourne in Sussex raises the question, did the Romans introduce topiary to England? They can scarcely have introduced the cypress. The existence here of box is, however, a problem. It has long been regarded as native. Yet there is a considerable area in northern France where it is not native, making a gap between the main natural distribution in Europe and that in the British Isles. Professor Godwin in his *History of the English Flora* remarks on its association in England with Roman burial sites—the shrub having played an important part in their funerary rites—and suggests that the Romans might have introduced it. If for funerals, why not for topiary, now that we know that they had such highly developed gardens?

The art of topiary therefore seems to have originated in Rome and been executed at least principally in Mediterranean cypress and box. The latter has now been with us so long as to be regarded as a native; it was mentioned, for example, by Turner in 1548, who called it by its present name, box. It gives its name to Boxley in Kent, Boxwell in the south Cotswolds, and Box Hill near Dorking. Otherwise, it is very local in its distribution and almost always seems to have arisen from planted trees (the hard wood was once valued by the wood-engraver and from it were made such articles as combs). It is usually a large shrub rather than a tree, and is immensely variable in its cultivated forms—dwarf, variegated leaved, and so on. The American Boxwood Society records no less than 102 names for these. The dwarf forms in particular have for centuries been used for edging parterres, flower borders and similar work. It has the power of thriving on all kinds of soils except those that are waterlogged, and is hardy.

Cypress has all the qualities needed by the topiarist—free growth (in Somerset it has reached 70 feet), tolerance of severe pruning, an attractive colour, ability to grow on soils with a high lime content—but it is not reliably hardy throughout the British Isles; it may live for many years and then be instantly killed by a freak of severe weather, even in the milder counties. It is doubtful if there are any old trees in Britain. In the Mediterranean region there are trees traditionally, but often dubiously, many centuries old and of great height and girth.

The pioneer botanist William Turner reported that it was growing at Syon House in 1548. Gerard in 1597 mentions it at the same place, at Greenwich, and Hampstead "in the garden of Mr Wade". Parkinson in his *Paradisi in Sole Paradisus Terrestris* (1629) wrote of it "for the goodly proportion* this tree beareth, as also for its evergreen head, it is and hath been of great account with all Princes, both beyond and on this side of the sea, to plant them in rowes on both sides of some spatious walk, which by reason of their high growing, and little spreading, must be planted the thicker together, and so they give a goodly, pleasant and sweet shadow: or else alone, if they have not many, in the middle of some quarter, or as they think meete. The wood thereof, of a brown yellow colour, and of a strong, sweete smell, whereof chestes or boxes are made to keepe apparell, linnen, furres and other things, to preserve them from moths and to give them a good smell."

There is nothing to suggest that it was grown to be clipped into fancy shapes. Yet it was clearly considered to be a formal, decorative tree in gardens.

In 1662 we come to our first authoritative work on trees, John Evelyn's *Sylva*. By now the court and its intelligentsia had spent an enforced visit to the continent of Europe and seen the great formal gardens of Le Nôtre and others. He has much to say about the cypress and topiary.

"Cupressus, the cypress-tree", he tells us, is of two kinds, the pyramidal and beautiful, and the other, called somewhat preposterously the male, of a more extravagant shape. He goes on at some length to explain that only a few years ago it was reported to be tender, only cultivated with greatest care, "whereas we see it now in every garden, rising to as goodly a bulk and stature as most you will find even in Italy itself". He goes on to explain its cultivation and training, and how the cruel frosts in the years 1663 and 1665 killed only three or four of a thousand growing in his garden. He urges its use for hedges and topiary . . . but it was false optimism, as the carefully observant and distinguished botanist John Ray in his *Historia Plantarum* (1686) describes how the cypresses in England were almost entirely exterminated by the frosts of 1683–4.

The Mediterranean cypress was undoubtedly used here both for hedges and topiary—particularly for spirals. In 1611, 200 "sypris trees at one shilling the peece" were imported from Paris for the new garden at Hatfield; in 1659 Sir Thomas

* I take it that we should today say "for its good form".

RIGHT: *Hypnerotomatica Polyphili*—
'Topiare woorke' (page 19)

BELOW: Knots from
Parkinson's *Paradisi* 1629 (page 24)

ABOVE: The yew tunnel, Melbourne, Derbyshire (page 40)

LEFT: The 17th–century small clipped yews at Powis Castle today (page 39)

BELOW: A garden from John James's *Theory and Practice of Gardening* 1712 (page 33)

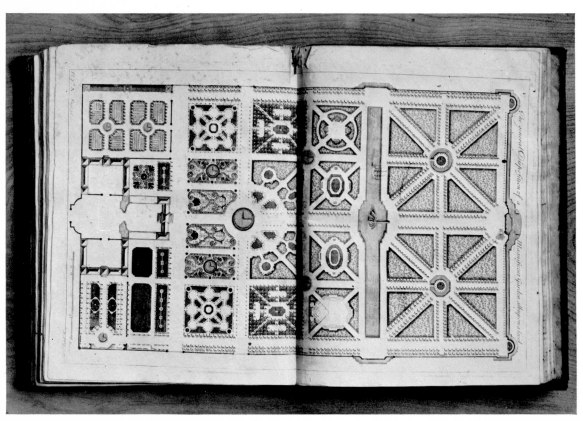

Hanmer remarked that of late years, though tender, it had been much propagated from seed borne in this country; in 1691 the nurseryman Pearson of Hoxton was selling 3 foot trees in quantities, and Alexander Pope grew them (but untrimmed) in his garden.

Topiary in Britain on the grand scale had no great success until it was eventually formed—as it is today—from our native yew, a tree with almost as much legend with us as has the cypress in the Mediterranean. Box has usually been the material for our small-scale work.

YEW AND HOLLY

Yew, holly, and Scots pine are the only evergreen natives of the British Isles that normally grow to tree size. This shortage has from early times led to the introduction of exotic evergreens. In the seventeenth and eighteenth centuries a gardener's collection of "greens" and their condition—with bright, clean, shiny leaves of rich colour—were one test of his success as a horticulturist. The introduction of, particularly western North American, conifers has during the last century or so entirely altered the aspect of our wintry countryside from one of leaflessness to one of rich greens.

The yew, *Taxus baccata*, is a native of Europe, Africa, and western Asia. In Britain it is scattered as a wild tree in woodlands and scrub from Perth and Argyll southwards. It is commonest on sharply drained limestone and chalk soils, very rarely forming pure woods which are usually on such sites. It is often found in deciduous woodland because it will tolerate shade. It has long been planted, particularly in churchyards, and self-sown seedlings from cultivated trees are common. It will thrive in any soil or situation that is well drained; that is vital for it. It is wind firm and hardy.

The sexes are—with very rare exceptions—on different trees. The very numerous male flowers are minute balls which shed their pollen in clouds, perhaps as early as February in a mild season. This drifts in the breeze on to the insignificant green female flowers which develop into the crimson yew berries, each of which carries a seed. These are distributed by the birds that eat the fleshy part and excrete the stones. Rarely, the berries are a rich yellow.

The thin, scaly bark when scraped or brushed away shows a rich cinnamon inner bark which is of a satiny texture and very beautiful.

The foliage, particularly when it has been lying on the ground after pruning and got somewhat dried, must be regarded as very poisonous to livestock. It is dangerous to regard a limited number of apparent exceptions to this rule as valid. The berries are poisonous to humans.

It has an unusual feature in the manner of its growth. On ageing, it throws up circumferential stems from the base which gradually unite, the original trunk in time rotting and resulting in a hollow centre. It is thus impossible to make a ring count, or obtain any wood from the centre to provide material for a radio-carbon estimate of its age. It is very tenacious of life. Old trees can be cut back to the bare trunk and will sprout freely. There are records of trees having been almost disintegrated when struck by lightning and surviving. Trees of considerable size and age have been successfully transplanted.

In Britain it is many centuries since trees of suitable size have been available for making bows—yet its traditional connection with war and death can be taken back to prehistoric times by the discovery of yew spears, one found at Clacton being of great antiquity and another in Lower Saxony being found between the ribs of the extinct straight-tusked elephants.

Why yews were planted in churchyards—usually one beside the path leading to the main doorway from the funeral entrance and another beside the path leading to the lesser doorway—is unknown. Sir Thomas Browne in his *Hydrotaphia* of 1658 wrote that whether it was so planted owing to its part in ancient funeral rites or because its perpetual verdure is symbolic of immortality "may admit conjecture"— it still does.

Decking churches with the foliage at Eastertide was continued until the last century.

It is surprising that such a tree, so abundant, so free-growing and so hardy, was not used from the earliest times as a substitute for the cypress in topiary and hedges which became so popular as our gardens developed on the Italian and French pattern—a fact proved by the negative evidence of its absence from many old garden plans and descriptions.

Again we must turn to Evelyn. One cannot forbear quoting that the typical utilitarian motives that he always adduces to encourage the planting of trees of all kinds:

> Since the use of bows is laid aside amongst us, the propagation of the yew tree (of which we have two sorts,* and other places reckon more, as the Arcadian black and red; the yellow of Ida, infinitely esteemed of old) is likewise quite forborn; but the neglect of it is to be deplored; seeing that (besides the rarity of it in Italy and France, where but little of it grows), the barrenest of our grounds and the coldest of our mountains . . . might be profitably replenished with them: I say, profitably, for, besides the use of the woods for bows . . . (for which the close and more deeply dyed is best) the forementioned artists in Box,† cabinet makers, inlayers and for the parquetè—floors,

* Does Evelyn here differentiate the male and female trees?
† He has previously described this, without reference to its use in topiary.

Yew covered promenade, Old Colwall, Herefordshire (page 40)

Elvaston Castle, 1881 (page 48)

Woolmers (page 49)

most gladly employ it; and in Germany they use to wainscot their stores with boards of this material; also for the cogs of mills, posts to be set in moist grounds, and everlasting axle-trees, there is none to be compared with it; likewise for the bodies of lutes, theorb's, bowls, wheels and pins for pullies; yea, and for tankards to drink out of . . .

But for our purpose, the following passage is the more important:

This English yew tree is easily produced of the seeds, washed and cleansed from their mucilage, then buried and dried in their sand a little moist, any time in December, and so kept in some vessel in the house all winter, and in some cool shady place abroad all the summer, sow them the spring after. Some bury them in the ground like haws. It will commonly be the second winter e'er they peep, and then they rise with their caps on their heads. Being three years old, you may transplant them, and form them into standards, knobs, walks, hedges, etc. in all which works they succeed marvellous well, and are worth our patience for their perennial verdure and durableness. I do again name them for hedges, preferably for beauty, and a stiff defence to any plant I have ever seen, and may upon that account (without vanity) be said to be the first which brought it into fashion, as well for defence, as a succedaneum for cypress, whether in hedges, or pyramids, conic-spires, bowls, or what other shapes, adorning the parks or other avenues with their lofty tops thirty foot high, and braving all the efforts of the most rigid winter, which cypress cannot weather. I have said how long-lasting they are, easily to be shaped and clipped; nay, cut down and revive: but those which are much superannuated, and perhaps of many hundred years standing, perish if so used.

In fact, Evelyn was not the first to employ yew for these purposes: There is a plan in the library of the Royal Institute of British Architects by John Smithson, who died in 1634, of a garden showing "yew trees cut into beasts". Nevertheless, as I have written earlier, English garden works in yew before the Restoration are significant by their absence from plans and descriptions. Evelyn was widely read and immensely influential. He can rightly be credited with originating the fashion, indeed craze (to some considerable extent encouraged later by the Dutch influence of William and Mary) for yew topiary that reigned in England until at least the death of Queene Anne, and has continued in moderation ever since.

Yew, then, is the tree on which British topiary exists.

If yew is the staple for topiary, holly has for long been famous for its use in ornamental hedges. Curiously, little seems to have been written about it before Evelyn's often quoted description:

Is there under *Heaven* a more glorious and refreshing Object of the Kind, than an impregnable *Hedge* of about *four hundred Foot* in *Length,* *nine* Foot *high,* and *five* in *Diameter*; which I can show in my now ruined *Gardens* at *Say's-Court* (thanks to the *Czar* of *Moscow*) at any Time of the Year, glittering with its armed and varnished *Leaves*? The taller *Standards* at orderly Distances, blushing with their natural *Coral*: It mocks at the rudest Assaults of the *Weather, beasts,* or *hedge-breakers* . . . It is with us of *two* eminent Kinds, the *prickly* and *smoother leaved*; or, as some term it, the *Free-Holly*, not unwelcome, when tender, to *Sheep* and other *Cattle*: There is also of the *White-berried,* and a *Golden* and *Silver*, variegated in six or seven Differences, which proceeds from no Difference from in the *Species*, but accidentally . . .

There seems no doubt that Evelyn mistook the adult form of foliage on old trees and at the tops of young trees of the common holly for another species: the almost spineless forms that are now cultivated not being known before 1838. He mentions the white-berried kind, as does Moses Cook, which is now unknown (and later in his account, the yellow-berried kind which he says, I think incorrectly, comes true from seed). He disbelieves the story that the variegated forms can be produced by raising plants in very poor soil mixed with chalk. We may continue with a lesser-known quotation which has a modern ring: and offers suggestions for today:

> I have seen *Hedges*, or if you will, stout *Walls* of *Holly* twenty foot in height, kept upright, and the *gilded* sort budded low, and in two or three places one above another, shorn and fashioned into *Columns* and *Pilasters, architectionally* shap'd, and at due distance; than which nothing can possibly be more pleasant, the *Berry* adorning the *Intercolumniations* with the *scarlet Festoons* and *Encarpa*.

CHAPTER 2

Topiary comes to Britain

EARLY EXAMPLES

Probably the earliest recorded example of topiary work in Britain is found in the description of Hampton Court when, Henry VIII took it over, and that rapacious monarch began to enlarge the gardens. In 1533 the "mount" was built. These mounts were features of large gardens consisting usually of some sort of seat or arbour set on a pile of earth rising well above the level of the garden so that the owner could look around the landscape in general and his own estate in particular. The top was reached by a path spiralling up which was usually bordered with a low hedge and was itself usually planted with shrubs.

At Hampton Court a pile of a quarter of a million bricks was covered with soil and planted with hawthorns. On its summit was a many-windowed building. The path up was bordered by stone heraldic beasts and no doubt some sort of clipped hedge, as was described by the King's antiquary, John Leland, when he visited Wressel Castle, near Howden in Yorkshire in 1540: "The gardens within the mote, and the orchardes without, were exceeding fair. And yn the orchardes were mounts, *opere topiario*, written about with degrees like the turnings in cokil shelles, to come to the top without payn."

This suggests that the craft of topiary was understood and practised in Britain well before that year.

The *Oxford Dictionary* has as its earliest English reference to the word "Topiary" a quotation from the translation (1592) of Fra Francesco Colonna's *Hypnerotomatica Polyphili*—a famous example of early printing published by Aldus in 1499. This reads, "By turnyng down the transomes, did join decently one with the other with a Topiarie woorke (From the French *topiairie*, Rabelais, 1548)." This English translation has a marginal note, "Topiaria, the feate of making of arbours in trees."

Colonna's work was also known from its translation as *Le Songe de Polyphile* by

Beroalde de Verville published in Paris in 1600. This has designs differing from the original one.

The suggestion that the craft of topiary came to us through France is, perhaps, confirmed by another early reference, which also refers to other forms of ornamental "woodwork" then found in gardens. The Gascon poet Guillaume de Salluste du Bartas, who died in 1590, wrote *La première Semaine, ou la Création*. Joshuah Sylvester (1563–1618) translated this, and has the following passage describing the garden of Eden:

> *Heer, underneath a fragrant Hedge reposes,*
> *Full of all kinds of sweet all-coloured Roses*
> *Which (one would think) the Angels daily dresse*
> *In true love-knots, tri-angle, lozenges.*
>
> > *Anon he walketh in a levell lane,*
> *On eyther side beset with shady Plane,*
> *Whose archèd boughs for* Frize *and* Cornich *bear*
> *Thick Groves, to change from future change of air:*
> *Then in a path impal'd, in pleasant wise,*
> *With sharp-sweet Orange, Lemon, Citron trees;*
> *Whose leavie twigs, that intricately tangle,*
> *Seem painted wals, whereon true fruits do dangle.**
>
> > *Now in plenteous Orchard planted rare*
> *With un-graft Trees, in checker round and square:*
> *Whose goodly fruits so on his will do wait,*
> *That plucking one, another ready's straight:*
> *And having tasted all (with due satiety)*
> *Finds all one goodness, but in taste variety.*
>
> > *Anon he stalketh with an easy stride,*
> *By some clear River's lilly-pavèd side,*
> *Whose sand's pure gold, whose pebbles precious Gemms,*
> *And liquid, silver all the curling streams:*
> *Whose chiding murmer, mazing in and out,*
> *With Crystall cisterns moats a mead about:*
>
> > *And th'artless Bridges, over-thwart this Torrent,*
> *Are rocks self-archèd by the eating Current:*
> *Or loving* Palms, *whose lusty Females willing*
> *Their marrow-boyling loves to be fulfilling*
> *(And reach their Husband-trees on th'other banks)*
> *Bow their stiffe backs, and serve for passing planks . . .*
> *Musing, anon through crooked walks he wanders,*

---

* In ancient and early gardens, decorative floral paintings seem to have been frequent—as for example in Livia's garden unearthed in Pompeii.

Round-winding rings, and intricate Meanders,
False guiding paths, doubtful beguiling strays,
And right-wrong errors of an endless Maze:
Not simply hedgèd with a simple border
Of Rosemary, *cut-out with curious order*
In Satyrs, Centaurs, Whales, *and* half-men-horses,
And thousand other counterfaited corses.

Here is a rich, exaggerated and glittering picture of the French gardens of the period of the great sixteenth-century French designer J. A. du Cerceau, and of which elements are to be found in such English poems as Skelton's *Garden of Laurel* and put to a considerable extent into practice at such gardens as Hampton Court, Nonsuch, Theobalds and Hatfield.

KNOTS AND PARTERRES: A NOTE

It will be as well at this stage to mention knots and parterres, which so often make use of dwarf and sometimes fancifully clipped hedges and which were an integral element of the gardens in which topiary played an important part. They will appear in greater detail later in the text.

A knot was a small rectangular bed. On it was outlined a pattern in box, rosemary, thrift or some low-growing plant. The patterns were usually but not always geometrical, frequently resembling the Dutch architectural designs known as strapwork. The spaces were filled in with coloured gravels, glittering spas—even shining black coal—or plants. The more elaborate the patterns in a knot garden (which would consist of a number of knots, each of a different kind) the more highly was it esteemed. The *Oxford Dictionary* informs us that the use of the word in this horticultural sense is first found in the late fifteenth century and appears to have been some sort of a maze.

The parterre, of which more will be said later, was really a complicated development of the knot, which reached its highest state of perfection in France during the era of Le Nôtre, gardener to Louis XIV. It was a consummate work of gardening (rather than truly horticultural) artifice. It became particularly fashionable in Britain with the return of Charles II and his Court from the Continent, where they had seen this type of work. It was not unknown before—being found in Commonwealth gardens.

In the eighteenth century British fashion turned against it. The Victorians revived its use, usually in crude form, and combined it with "bedding out"—the use of exotic half-hardy plants during the summer period only, or until the first frosts turned them into a flaccid mess.

LAWSON AND BACON

William Lawson in *The Countrie Housewife's Garden* (1617) and *A New Orchard and Garden* (1618) described enthusiastically and fancifully those parts of the garden which involved edgings, hedges and topiary.

> Let that which is said in the orchards form suffice for gardens in general: but for special forms in squares, they are as many, as there are devices in gardiner's brains. Neither is the wit and art of a skilful gardiner in this point not to be commended, that can work more variety for breeding of more delightsome choice, and of all those things where the owner is able and desirous to be satisfied. The number of forms, mazes and knots is so great, and men are so diversely delighted, that I leave every housewife to herself, especially seeing to set down many, had been to fill much paper; yet lest I deprive her of all right and direction, let her view these choice new forms; and note this generally, that all plots are square, and all are bordered with privit, raisins,* fea-berries,† roses, thorn, rosemary, bee-flowers,‡ hyssop, sage or such like.

The "forms" illustrated are the cink-foil, flower-de-luce, tre-foy, ret, lozenge, diamond, oval and maze. And elsewhere:

> Then in the corners of your orchard you have mounts of stone or wood, curiously wrought within and without, or of earth covered with fruit trees, Kentish cherries, damsons, plums, etc. with stairs of precious workmanship; and in some corner (or more) a true dial or clock, and some antick works; and especially silver-sounding musick, mixt instruments, and voices, gracing all the rest: how will you be wrapt with delight?
>
> Large walks, broad and long, close and open, like the Temp-groves in Thessaly, raised with gravel and sand, having seats and banks of camomile; all this delights the mind and brings health to the body.
>
> View now with delight the work of your own hands, your fruit-trees of all sorts, loaden with sweet blossoms, and fruit of all tastes, operations and colours: your trees standing in comely order, which way so ever you look. Your borders on every side hanging and dropping with feberries, raspberries, barberries, and the roots of your trees powdered with strawberries, red, white and green, what a pleasure is this! Your gardener can frame your lesser wood to the shape of men armed in the field, ready to give battle; of swift-running grey hounds, or of well-sented and true-running hounds to chase the deer, or hunt the hare. This kind of hunting shall not waste your corn, nor much your coyn.

* Figs.   † Gooseberry.   ‡ Wall-flowers.

Mazes well framed a man's height, may perhaps make your friend wandering in gathering of berries till he cannot recover himself without your help.

This account, surely tinged with exaggeration and fantasy, now and then echoing the prose of King James's *Bible* at least demonstrates the important part played by clipping and training and by the topiarist's art in Jacobean times.

Francis Bacon was the greatest intellect of the Jacobean era, with a wide-ranging mind that amazes to this day. His essay *Of Gardens* is but one of many which gave the most profound consideration to a multitude of topics. Published in 1625, it was about what, in his opinion, gardens should be like, not what they actually were. It has had at one time and another considerable influence on the usually rather shallow philosophy of gardening.

Apposite to our subject are his instructions for devising the "green", to which is assigned four acres:

The greene hath two pleasures; the one, because nothing is more pleasant to the eye, than greene grass kept finely shorne; the other, because it will give you a faire alley in the midst, by which you may go in front upon a *stately hedge*, which is to inclose the *garden*. But, because the alley will be long, and in great heat of the yeare or day, you ought not to buy the shade in the *garden*, by going in the sunne through the *greene*, therefore you are, of either side the *greene*, to plant a *covert alley*, upon carpenters works, about twelve foot in height, by which you may go in shade, into the garden.

As for the making of *knots* or *figures*, with divers coloured earths, that they may lie under the windowes of the house, on that side, which the garden stands, they be but *toyes*: you may see as good sights, many times, in tarts.

The *garden* is best to be square; incompassed on all four sides, with a stately *arched hedge*. The *arches* to be upon *pillars*, of carpenters worke, of some ten foot high, and six foot broad: and the spaces between, of the same dimension, with the breadth of the arch. Over the *arches* let there bee an *entire hedge*, of some foure foot high, framed also upon carpenters worke: and upon the *upper hedge*, over every *arch*, a little *turret*, with a *belly*, enough to receive a *cage* of *birds*: And over every *space*, between the *arches*, some other little *figure*, with broad plates of *round coloured glasse*, gilt, for the sunne to play upon. But this *hedge* I entend to be raised upon a *bancke*, not steepe, but gently slope, of some six foot, set all with *flowers*. Also, I understand, that this *square* of the *garden*, should not be the whole breadth of the ground, but to leave, on either side, ground enough for, diversity of *side alleys*: unto which, the two *covert alleys* of the *greene*, may deliver you. But there must be, no *alleys* with *hedges*, at either end, of this great *inclosure*: not at the *hither* end, for letting your prospect upon this faire hedge from the *greene*; nor at the *further end*, for letting your prospect from the hedge, through the arches, upon the *heath*.*

* This was more or less comparable with what we should today call a wild garden.

For the ordering of the ground within the *great hedge*, I leave it to variety of device; advising, nevertheless, that whatsoever forme you cast it into, first it be not too busie, or full of worke. Wherein I, for my part, do not like images cut out in juniper, or other *garden stuffe*: they be for children. *Little low hedges* round, like welts, and some pretty *pyramides*, I like well: and in some places, *faire columnes* upon frames of carpenters worke. I would also, have the *alleys*, spacious and faire. You may have *closer alleys* upon the *side grounds*, but none in the *maine garden*.

Bacon's suggestions seem to have been entirely original. I know of no contemporary or earlier treatise resembling this. In fact the simplicity and calm geometry of his proposals do not seem to have been carried out until late in the nineteenth and early in the present century. Designers of today would do well to study his writings and adopt his principles, though perhaps not his detail, to present conditions.

What was in reality being carried out in the first decades of the seventeenth century is seen in the next extract.

PARKINSON'S PARADISE

The first consequential book—and consequential it still is—devoted to British gardening was John Parkinson's *Paradisi in Sole Paradisus Terrestris* of 1629. From the section "A garden of all sorts of pleasant flowers which our English air will permit to be noursed up" we can learn about the dwarf hedges which bordered the knots. Omitting the herbs, such as thrift, once much used, whose bushy growth "doth hide and shelter snayles and other small noisome wormes so plentifully, that gilloflowers, and other fine herbes and flowers being planted therein, are much spoyled by them, and cannot be helped without much industry and very great and daily attendance to destroy them" he passes on to shrubs:

Lavender Cotton* being finely slipped† and set, is of many, and those of highest respect of late daies, both for the beauty and forme of the herbe, being of a whitish greene mealy colour, for his sent smelling somewhat strong, and being everliving and abiding greene all the winter, will, by cutting be kept in as even proportion as any other maybe. This will likewise soon grow great and stubbed, notwithstanding the cutting, and besides will now and then perish in some places, especially if you do not strike or put off the snow, before the sun lying upon it dissolve it. The rarity and novelty of this herbe, being for the most part but in the gardens of great persons, doth cause it to be of the greater

* *Santolina chamaecyparissus.*   † Rooted from slips (cuttings).

regard, it must therefore be renewed every second or third yeare at the most, because of the great growing thereof. Slips of juniper or yew are also received of some planted, because they are always green, and that the juniper especially hath not that ill sent that boxe hath, which I will presently commend unto you, yet both juniper and yew will soon grow too great and stubbed, and force you to take up your know sooner, than if it were planted with boxe, which lastly, I chiefly and above all other herbes commend unto you, and being a small, lowe or dwarfe kind, is called French or Dutch boxe, and soweth very well to set out any knot, or border any beds: for besides that it is ever greene, it being reasonable thicke set, will easily be cut and formed into any one fashion one will, according to the nature thereof, which is to grow very slowly, and will not in a long time rise to be of any height, but shooting forth many small branches from the roote, will grow very thicke, and yet not require so great tending, nor so much perish as any of the former, and is only received into the gardens of those that are curious.* This (as I before said) I command to bee the best and surest herbe to abide faire and greene in all the bitter stormes of the sharpest winter, and all the great heats and droughts of summer, and doth recompence the want of a good sweet sent with his fresh verdure, and long lasting continuance. Yet these inconveniences it hath, that besides the unpleasing sent which many mislike, and yet is but small, the rootes of this boxe do so much spread themselves into the ground of the knot, and do draw from thence so much nourishment, that it robbeth all the herbes that grow neare it of their sap and substance, therefore making all the earth about it barren, or at least lesse fertile. Wherefore to show you the remedy of this inconvenience of spreading without either taking up the boxe or the border, or the herbes and flowers in the knot, is I thinke a secret knowne but unto few, which is this: you shall take a broad pointed iron like unto a slise or chessill, which thrust downe right into the ground a good depth all along the inside of the border of boxe somewhat close thereunto, you may thereby cut away the spreading rootes thereof, which draw so much moisture from the other herbes on the inside, and by this meanes both preserve your herbes and flowers in the knot, and your boxe also, for that the boxe will be nourished sufficiently from the rest of the rootes it shooteth on all the other sides.

Then follows an account of the other materials suitable for edgings—from lead, tiles and blue pebbles to jaw-bones used beyond the seas but too gross for this country.

Finally, come the plants to

border the whole square or know about, to serve as a hedge thereunto, every one taketh what liketh him best; as either privet alone, or sweete bryer, and white thorne interlaced, and roses of one, or two, or more sorts placed here and there amongst them. Some also take lavender, rosemary, sage, southernwood, lavender cotton, or some such

* The meanings of this word in Parkinson's time were "careful, studious, attentive, fastidious, ingenious, eager to learn, taking the interest of a connoisseur in any branch of art" (*Oxford Dictionary*).

other thing. Some againe plant cornell trees* and plash them, or keepe them lowe, to forme them into an hedge. And some againe take a lowe prickly shrubbe, that abideth always greene, described in the end of this book, called in Latine *Pyracantha*, which in time will make an evergreen hedge or border, and when it beareth fruit, which are red berries like unto hawthorne berries, make a glorious show among the greene leaves in the winter time, when no other shrubbes have fruit or leaves.

A notable absentee from these lists is yew. When we come to it in the main body of the work, we read only that "it is found planted both in the corners of orchards, and against the windowes of houses, to be both a shadow and an ornament, in being always greene, and to deck up houses in winter, but ancient writers have ever reckoned it to be dangerous at the least, if not deadly".

Parkinson refers also a to form of box which he calls *Buxus aurea*, the gilded box: "There is another kinde hereof but lately come to our knowledge, which differeth not anything from the former† but that all the leaves have a yellow list or gard about the edge of them on the upperside, and none on the lower, which maketh it sceme very beautiful; and is therefore called gilded boxe."‡

* *Cornus mas.*   † The "boxe tree".   ‡ *Buxus sempervirens* 'Aurea Marginata'.

CHAPTER 3

The Restoration and the Grand Manner

THE RESTORATION

With the coming of the troubles popularly associated with Cavaliers and Round-heads, little was written about gardens, though contrary to some usually held opinions, the Commonwealth was not a time when horticulture languished. Some of Cromwell's associates were distinguished botanical gardeners, and a number of Royalists retired to their country estates and gardens, to which they devoted time that would have been otherwise spent in Court life.

The Earl of Pembroke's magnificent Wilton House was largely built (or rather re-built) in Cromwell's time, though the original garden* was laid out by Isaac de Caux a little earlier, in 1632. Great use was made of clipped trees. The poet, John Taylor, refers particularly to this in his contemporaneous "Of the Gardens at Wilton":

Amongst the rest, the pains and industry of an ancient gentleman, Mr Adrian Gilbert, must not be forgotten: for he hath (much to my Lord's cost and his own pains) used such a deal of intricate setting, grafting, planting, inoculating, railing, hedging, plash-ing, turning, winding, and returning, circular, triangular, quadrangular, orbicular, oval, and every way curiously and chargeably conceited: then hath he made walks, hedges, and arbours, of all manner of most delicate fruit-trees, planting and placing them in such admirable art-like fashions, resembling both divine and moral remembrances, as three arbours standing in a triangle, having each a recourse to a greater arbour in the midst, resembleth three in one and one in three: and he hath there planted certain walks and arbours all with fruit trees, so pleasing and ravishing to the sense, that he calls it *Paradise*, in which he plays the part of a true Adamist, continually toiling and tilling.

Moreover, he hath made his walks most rarely round and spacious, one walk with-out another (as the rinds of an onion are greatest without, and less towards the centre),

* Much altered from 1700 onwards. It seems that de Caux's garden included the earliest known cedar of Lebanon planted in England.

and withall, the hedges betwixt each walk are so thickly set that one cannot see through from the one walk, who walks in the other: that, in conclusion, the work seems endless; and that in England, it is not to be followed, or will in haste be followed.

John Evelyn comes into his full glory immediately after the Restoration. Yet, in confirmation that gardening was much practised in Cromwellian times, he wrote in his diary on January 17th, 1653:

> I began to set out the ovall garden at Sayes Court, which was before a rude orchard and all the rest one intire field of 100 acres, without any hedge, except the hither holly hedge joyning to the Bank of the mount walk. This was the beginning of all the succeeding gardens, walks, groves, enclosures, and plantations there.

Of interest, and indicating the passion for evergreens that was to affect, and indeed still affects, the British owing to nature's niggardly dispensation of them to us, is an account of a visit Evelyn paid to Box Hill in 1655:

> I went to Box-hill to see those rare natural bowers, cabinets, and shady walks in the box copses: hence we walk'd to Mickleham, and saw Sir F. Stidolph's seate . . . Here are such goodly walkes and hills as render the place extreamly agreeable, it seeming from these ever-greens to be summer all the winter.

From 1642 until he settled at Sayes Court he had been abroad, observed and learned, noting in his diary, a great deal about European gardens, which after the Restoration he applied publicly rather than privately. By 1665 Pepys was able to write that his gardens were, "for variety of evergreens, and hedge of holly, the finest things I ever saw in my life".

In 1662 came Evelyn's *Silva*, the first outstanding British work on trees. Brought about by the shortage of oak for our navy, it ranged far beyond the brief given to the newly-formed Royal Society which in effect was responded to by Evelyn alone. The principal necessary quotations have already been made from this work. In 1693 he published the headings of his *Plan for a Royal Garden*, only one of which, that called "Acetaria, A Discourse on Sallets", materialized. Among the other proposed chapter headings which interest us are these:

> VII Of knots, trayle work, parterres, compartiments, borders, banks and embossments.
> VIII Of groves, labyrinths, dedals,* cabinets, cradles, close walks, galleries, pavilions, porticos, lanterns, and other relievos of topiary and hortulan architecture.

The use of clipped greens and shrubs certainly played a very important part in the Restoration garden.

* An obsolete word meaning maze.

Evelyn was an astonishing man, yet it is as well to remember what his friend, the Earl of Haddington,* said about him: ". . . he was too credulous, and regarded the age of the moon too much, and other niceties too trifling for so grand a man."

It is therefore interesting to turn to another contemporary of Evelyn's, Moses Cook, "Gardiner to the Earl of Essex at Cashiobury", a man of great practical experience and, as we now know, with views far in advance of most of his contemporaries.

He describes the plants used for ornamental hedging: "Juniper I take to be one of the best to make a low hedge, of any plant or tree we have in England: for it grows naturally very thick, is a slow grower, and hath always a fresh green colour, and the severest of our hard winters will not make it change its countenance." He adds that it is "something ticklish to be remov'd", but that he has succeeded in doing it

a little after *Bartholomew*-Tide (September) I did not lose one plant in ten; but they do flourish in to little hedges most gallantly . . .

Holly makes a most stately and beautiful hedge; and had we but store of the white-berry'd holly† to mix in the hedge with the red, it would make it the more ornamental. Its ground that it most delight on, is dry and gravelly. . . . Had we but store of the striped (variegated) to make hedges with, it would be very noble indeed.

Hornbeam may be kept in good shape for a high hedge, and very thick, even to the ground. It is (alone) one of the very best home-bred natural forest trees that shed the leaf to make a hedge of, and is fencible, unless against the rudest sort of cattel.

Box maketh a good hedge, and lasting; I mean the *English*, though the others are pretty, both the gilded and the dwarf.

Laurel (as we call it) or bay-cherry‡, make a good hedge; and if well kept, very fine standards. Hard winters do pierce it on some grounds, but on most it is durable: it is easy to increase, and will grow well on most grounds; keep it but down, and it will grow strong below, and thick, and then make a very fine hedge.

Arbutus, or strawberry-tree, is a curious plant for a hedge, only it is very tender, especially . . . while young, for the leaves being constant, whilst life lasteth, and of a fair green, finely dented about the edges, and its pretty white in flower in summer, with its strawberry on, the beginning of winter, all together add a great deal of grace to this plant.

Cypress would make fine hedges, but for two faults: for first, in some grounds it is tender, and will not abide our hard winters; and secondly, it doth not love to be headed, for that makes it still more tender. Cut it not in late summer.

---

* See page 44.
† I have never heard or read of this; the distinctively yellow-berried variety *bacciflava* is not uncommon in nature.
‡ *Prunus laurocerasus*.

Mezereon, or Dwarf-Bay, both the red and the white together, make a pretty low hedge, and show very beautifully early in the spring.

Rhamnus alaternus, or evergreen Privet, makes a fine thick green hedge: it should be supported with a frame, especially when it is young.

Pyracantha, or prickly Coral, makes a good thick hedge, and a very fine show when it is full of its fine red berries, which appear like beads of red coral among the dark green leaves. It likes our entertainment so well, that it will grow well on most grounds; our winters disturb it not, and 'tis very easy to be multiply'd or increas'd by laying or cutting.

They that have store of ground, and are lovers of plants, I hope will not be without these few named, and many more that will be very acceptable; but they are not, some of them, so proper for hedges. Many more there be that would make very fine hedges for pleasures, if well kept; as the double-blossom Cherry, the *Laurus Tinus*, or wild Bay, Primme, Savin, etc. [The mention of "double-flowering cherry" is perplexing: *Prunus avium* "Plena" is a large tree that dislikes pruning. Primme is an old name for privet, *Ligustrum vulgare*. Savin is *Juniperus sabina*.]

These few are only for ornament, and make (any of them), fine hedges alone; or you may mix them with judgement, and they will then be very pleasant.

Now I shall show you a few of those that are for profit and ornament; such are the Summer-Pears on Quince-stocks;* for that makes them the more dwarfish. Cherries make a fine hedge, but especially the small-leaved, and the several sorts of Flanders, etc.

Plumbs, Quinces, Codlins, Barberries, etc., all these make fine hedges, but must have supporters. In the three last there is this fault, that the better they be kept, I mean the handsomer, the worse they will bear.

Cassiobury was undoubtedly a wonderful garden, and Cook repeatedly demonstrates in his writing that he was a highly skilled gardener. We must take his views as those typical of his period. This was borne out in 1681 when, his employer having got into political trouble, he became one of the original partners in the nursery firm that later, under London and Wise, dominated British gardens and their design.

The parterre (of which mention has already been made) was so intimate a part of gardens in the great age of groves, topiary, arbours, and hedges that the description of it written by A. J. D. d'Argenville and published as *La Théorie et la Pratique du Jardinage* in 1709 is worth repeating. Particularly is this so as the delightful English translation by the architect John James, *The Theory and Practice of Gardening*, published in 1712 with "so great a number of subscriptions to it from both Houses of Parliament", included the owners of the most important gardens of the day:

The name of parterre has its original from the Latin word *partiri, to divide*; and according to some, a parterre denotes a flat and eaven surface.

* English gardeners at this period were, it seems, well known for their success with growing pears on the dwarfing quince stocks.

The compartiments and borders of parterres are taken from geometrical figures, as well right-lined, as circular, mix'd, etc. They take various designs into their composition, as branch'd and flourish'd work, palms, foliage, hawks-bills, springs, tendrells, volutes, knots, stalks, ties, chaplets, beads, husks, cartoozes, plumes, compartiments, frets or interlacings, wreaths and shell-works of grass, paths borders, etc. And sometimes to these are added the designs of flowers, as roses, pinks, tulips and the like.

Formerly they put in the heads of greyhounds, griffins and other beasts, with their paws and talons; which had a very ill effect, and made parterres look very heavy and clouterly.

The designs we see now-a-days are quite different; and 'tis pretended, that to have embroidery look well, it should be light, regular, and not confused; which often occasions the falling into the contrary fault to what they were in heretofore; and, out of a studious endeavour to make parterres appear light and free, they make them utterly unfurnish'd, and with an embroidery so thin meager, that it makes no figure upon the ground; but in four or five years time you are obliged to pull it up again, the edges of box coming to touch and interfere one with another. A just mean should be observed in things of this kind, equally avoiding too great a slenderness, as well as too great a massyness of ornaments.

There are divers sorts of parterres, which may be all reduced to these four that follow; namely, parterres of embroidery, parterres of compartiment, parterres after the English manner, and parterres of cut-work. There are also parterres of water, but at present they are quite out of use.

We need go no further into details except to add that

Parterres after the English manner are the plainest and meanest of all. They should consist only of large grass plots all of a pice, or cut but little, and be encompassed with a border of flowers, separated by a path of two or three foot wide, laid smooth, and sanded over, to make the greater distinction. We give it the name of *Parterre à l'Angloise*, because we had the manner of it first from England.

It is nice to read of the traditional English restraint being accepted at least to some extent by the French. From this delightful description, we can learn a good deal of the setting in which the great topiary gardens were set.

To compare with this Anglo-French list, Mr David Green, in *Gardener to Queen Anne*,* reproduces a most interesting list in manuscript of the trees used by Henry Wise. For our purpose, the evergreens are of considerable interest, and their names, all given in English, present several problems. These evergreens include trees which may be planted in "woodworks", being mixed with large forest trees, or used in avenues, "walks of shade" and hedges. The narrow-leaved trees and shrubs

* This account of Henry Wise is by far the most valuable study of the London and Wise era.

are "Yews" (*Taxus baccata*), "Silver Fir" (*Abies alba*), "Spruce Fir" (*Picea abies*), "Scotch Fir" (*Pinus sylvestris*), the "Cedar of Lebanon" (*Cedrus libani*), "Arbor Vitae" (*Thuya occidentalis*) and "Cyprus" (*Cupressus sempervirens*). We then come to what may be regarded as a heading ,"Juniper": that is obviously *Juniperus communis suecica*), and then come what amounts to a series of adjectives; "Goa" is what was generally known as Cedar of Goa (now *Cupressus lusitanica*) or the Mexican cypress, which possibly got its name because it was introduced to India by Catholic friars; it is known to have been in cultivation here in 1682. Then comes "Virginia", which is clearly *Juniperus virginiana* or the so-called pencil cedar, said to have been introduced by Evelyn in the mid-seventeenth century. "Bermuda" follows this—*Juniperus bermudiana*, not a hardy tree, but known to have been grown here in 1684; no doubt was kept in the greenhouse and stood out in summer. "New England" is a puzzle: *J. virginiana* is the only species which was grown here at that time. Evelyn also mentions "New England juniper", and the reference can only be to *J. communis*, a tree with an extraordinarily wide natural distribution, indeed, wider than any other tree or shrub, which is occasionally arborescent in New England. "Lycion" is another puzzle, until we find Evelyn referring to "the oxycedrus of Lycia", which must be the Mediterranean *J. oxycedrus*, or prickly juniper. The standard work on conifers gives the date of introduction of this as 1739. Wise died in 1738, and though the date of his list is not known, it suggests that it was made rather late in his life, while the fact that Evelyn names it surely means that it was grown here before the usually accepted date of introduction.

The "broad-leaved evergreen trees and shrubs" present only one problem. The first two items are merely "striped" and "plain". One can only assume that "hollies" has been omitted, as this in its several forms was very popular. The next item "evergreen oaks" does not help us, as there is no record of a variegated *Quercus ilex*; the plural is justified because this species varies a good deal in the shape and size of its leaf. The remainder are easily identified. "Laurels" will be *Prunus laurocerasus*, and probably the then newer *P. lusitanica*; "Bays", *Laurus nobilis*; "Laurustinus several sorts", *Viburnum tinus* and its variants; "Arbutus", *Arbutus unedo*; "Alaturnus several sorts", *Rhamnus alaternus* and no doubt its variegated kinds; "Phyllarda" must be a mis-spelling of the then popular *Phillyrea* species and variants; "Tree Sea Purslane", *Atriplex halimus*, now grown usually only as a seaside shrub but once popular; "Box", *Buxus sempervirens*; "Ivy", *Hedera helix*; "Pyracanthus", *Pyracantha coccinea*, and "Spurge Laurel", *Daphne laureola*.

Many of these will be found in the lists of plants suitable for clipping given at the end of this book. They were the subjects of "verdant sculpture" which, in the words of Horace Walpole, "had gone on till London and Wise had stocked our gardens with giants, animals, monsters, coats-of-arms and mottoes. . . ."

The ericetum at Woburn (page 50)

RIGHT: Country topiary—
horse and jockey (page 49)

BELOW: Shrubland Park
with its original parterres (page
57)

ENGLAND AND FRANCE

Gardening in the British Isles, though since Tudor times affected in a rather provincial manner by the practice in France, did not fully enter into the main European stream derived from Italy and developed in the grandest manner in France by designers culminating in André le Nôtre (1613–1700) until the English Court, with its brilliant intellectual members, was in exile on the Continent until the Restoration. The influence of France and Holland was, indeed, felt before that period—for example, when an exile such as John Evelyn, whom we have already mentioned, returned in 1653. But from the return of Charles II to the reign of Queen Anne was a period in which very many, often grandiose, gardens in the formal manner were laid out. The extent and magnitude of these is shown in the numerous topographical drawings of Leonard Knyff, born at Haarlem in 1650, who became a naturalized Englishman in 1694. Some of these were, no doubt, to some extent what his patron had in mind, but many, such as his view of Chatsworth in 1699, were accurate. From our point of view, there is in these huge schemes, among the thousands of trees and shrubs employed, not a single one that was not cut into shape: the shears dominated natural growth, just as did the architect with his geometry—we can recall Evelyn's admiring use of the word *architectonial*.

The dominant figure in garden design during this period was George London. Little is known of his origins or private life, except that he died in about 1713, and as a young man came to the notice of John Rose, the royal gardener, who took him to France, to which country he made further visits (studying the methods of Le Nôtre), as well as to Holland. He founded the firm of nurserymen, later to become London and Wise, and at Brompton built up an enormous stock of and business in evergreens, formerly supplied almost entirely from Holland, which country was famed for its topiary. The fashion for these was increased with the arrival of William and Mary. London travelled round the country, designing, and Wise at first stopped principally at Brompton, though he was later to design the original gardens at Blenheim, which had little resemblance to those now there.

There is plenty of evidence that the gardens were designed as part, or an extension of, the house; London, for example, is known to have worked with Talman.

The connection between house and garden was made clear by James, whose translation of d'Argenville is the nearest we can get to Le Nôtre's teaching. He went so far as to say that the size of the house should be related to the size of the garden.

It is better, therefore, to be content with a reasonable spot of ground, well cultivated, than to be ambitious of having parks to such extent, that three quarters of them are ordinarily neglected. The true size for a handsome garden, may take in 30 or 40 acres not more. As to the building, which generally swallows up half the expense, there is no necessity that it should be so large and so magnificent, tho' many stand upon it to have palaces, and to be lodg'd better in the country than in the town. One may justly say, that a building in the country should be proportioned to the extent of its garden: for it could be fully as disagreeable, to see a magnificent building in a little garden, as a small box in a garden of vast extent. These are two extremes which should be equally avoided, by making the building correspond with the garden, and the garden with the building.

These proportions having been decided, we are asked to observe the general rules in the disposition and distribution of the gardens.

The first rule is that the house should be at least a little above the garden, and so looking down on to the parterre, by now an elaborate design, full of colour.

The shrubs used in these parterres were called *arbustes* and included "the common and Persian lilaches, the Dutch and monthly rose-trees, honeysuckles, syringas, common jasmine and jonquils, privet, sweet trefoil, rosemary, Spanish broom, etc., which shrubs are so well known by everyone, that I shall make no description of them in this place". It is not easy today to decide precisely what all these were.

James continues: "To accompany parterres, we make choice of those designs of wood-work* that are most delicate, as groves opened in compartments, quin-cunxes,† verdant-halls, with bowling greens,‡ arbour-work, and fountains in the-middle. These small groves are so much more agreeable near a house, in that you presently find shade, without going far to seek it; besides, they communicate a coolness to the apartments, which is very much coveted in hot weather."

This reminds us that a garden in a continental climate is being described, and we realize that this carefully clipped and trained "wood-work" is of deciduous trees—in fact, hornbeam, maple, elm, "oaklings" and sweet chestnuts, kept headed to ensure a tufted growth at their base.

That this is so is emphasized by what follows: "It would be of use to plant some small groves of evergreens, that you might have the pleasure of seeing a wood always verdant in the very coldest reasons. They would look very well when seen from the building, and I earnestly recommend the planting of some squares of them in a handsome garden, to make a diversity of the other wood; which, having lost its leaves, appears quite naked all the winter." Here, as elsewhere, we must read "wood" in the sense of groups of trees.

---

* This perhaps misleading word means the use of carefully clipped trees.

† The arrangement of, say, four trees at the corner of a square with a fifth at its centre, the ground below being bare.

‡ A translation of *boulingrin*—not, in fact, a green on which to play bowls, but a small sunken area of grass with sloping sides.

The evergreens ordinarily made use of in these gardens were:

The yew, one of the finest evergreens; it grows as tall or as low as you please; and, in a wood, may be brought to any form, by clipping . . . its branches very full of leaves, of a deep green, and extremely pleasant to the eye. It is fit for pallisades, as also for garnishing the borders of parterres. 'Tis pretended, that its shade is very dangerous and unwholesome.*

The picea, or pitch-tree, is pretty much like the yew in its wood and its leaf, but it shoots up much higher, and does not grow so handsome, nor so thick of branches as the yew does. It is proper only in woods, and in great double walks, when 'tis planted between the detached trees. They make no use of it now-a-days in parterres, because it grows too high, and is very subject to be unfurnished at foot. . . .

The fir-tree is one of those that rise the highest and straightest of any. . . . Its leaves are much like those of the yew; it is fit only for woods and forests, and especially for hilly places. . . .

The pine is a tree very different from the fir, though many people confound one with the other. It shoots up very high, and pretty upright. It puts out abundance of branches which are very full of leaves above, and quite naked below. . . . Its fruit is called the pine-apple.†

The cypress is a very beautiful tree, and rises to a great height. It is furnished very thick from its foot to its very top, which terminates in a point . . . its leaves, which are of whitish green, are very thick; it is proper for making alleys and pallisades.

The scarlet-oak,‡ or holm, somewhat resembles an apple-tree or pear-tree; it does not rise to high as the common oak, and its wood is very different, but its leaves and acorn are much like it, except that they are smaller and a light green. This tree is proper to make walks of, and its species is perpetual by the acorn it bears.

Then follows a list of the shrubs and plants used to form palisades, to furnish the lower parts in woods of evergreens and to set off the borders of parterres.

The holly passes for one of the finest ever-green shrubs that are to be met with . . .
    The juniper tree shoots pretty high, and smells very well . . .
    The Phillyrea is a shrub that does not rise very high: its wood is blackish, and its leaves resemble those of the olive, but are shorter, and of a tolerable good green. This

---

* An unfounded claim made by several classical authors.
† It is this pine cone, not the tropical fruit, which is usually sculpted in ornaments.
‡ *The Garden Book of Sir Thomas Hanmer* (1659) describes "The Scarlet Oak. In Latin called *Ilex coggirea,* called scarlet not from the colour of the wood, or leaves, which are greene at all times, but from a certaine excrescence growing to some trees, wherein wormes are bred and a graine of which a perfect scarlet colour is made." This is *Querus coccifera* the Kermes Oak, a Mediterranean species. It is possibly confused here with the now much commoner evergreen or or holm oak, *Querus Ilex. Q. coccifera* seldom is more than a large bush in the British Isles; at that time *Q. ilex* was not often grown.

shrub grows very well furnish'd, which makes it esteemed for palisades; it grows
without difficulty even in the shade . . .

Sabin, or savine, grows very tall for a shrub; its stem is somewhat bulky . . . its
leaves are like the cypress-tree . . .

The pyracantha, which the French call *Le buisson ardent,* is pretended to be the same
with that, in which scripture tells us God appears to Moses. It does not grow very tall,
and its leaf is very much like that of the plum tree. Its red berries, which continue on it
in the winter, making it look as though it were full of fire, have given it the name of the
Burning Bush . . .

The alaternus resembles the olive-tree in its leaves; they are of a blackish green, and
pretty thick; it is very fit to make palisades with . . .

The box-tree is a green shrub of the greatest use, and one of the most necessary in
gardens. There are two sorts of it; the dwarf-box, which the French call *Buis d'Artois,*
the leaves of which are like those of the myrtle, but greener and harder. This is made
use of for planting the embroidery of parterres, and the edgings of borders. It naturally
does not grow very much, which makes it called dwarf-box. The other kind is the box-
tree of the woods, which advances much higher, and has bigger leaves than the former,
which makes it fit to form palisades, and green tufts for garnishing of woods; it comes
up in the shade, but is a long time gaining any considerable height . . .

These, the author concludes, are all the trees and shrubs that are ordinarily made
use of in fine gardens, those that are clipped and trained, or, as used to be said,
subjected to the tonsile arts.

Though outside our scope, it is interesting to add a description of the large trees
grown primarily for their height and erect growth "to form handsome walks".

They are "elms, limes and horse-chesnuts. Walks of elms, when well kept, grow
very tall and lofty; they put out beautiful leaves and are withal very lasting.*
Walks of limes are likewise very handsome, especially when they are Dutch limes;
these trees are known to shoot up very high, they have a smooth bark, a most agreeable leaf and yield an abundance of flowers that smell very sweet; besides which,
they are subject to no sort of vermin.† These are the two kinds of trees I advise
you constantly to make use of, preferably to the horse-chesnut,‡ notwithstanding
it is so much in fashion. I cannot deny but the horse-chesnut is a handsome tree;
'tis certain it grows very upright, has a fine body, a polish'd bark, and a beautiful

---

* These were not the same as our hedgrow elms, usually grown in British avenues, which are
Ulmus procera (campestris), native only of the British Isles, but *U. carpinifolia,* the smooth-
leaved elm, which in fact is called by Evelyn in *Sylva* the French elm.

† The Dutch lime is the hybrid *Tilia europaea;* it is, in fact, often badly affected by aphides.

‡ *Aesculus hippocastanum* was brought to France from Constantinople in 1615. Cardinal Riche-
lieu, who died in 1645, planted it extensively at Rueil, as did Le Nôtre in his great schemes
a little later. London and Wise made great use of it for avenues at, among other places, Hampton
Court and Windsor from 1699 on; some still survive.

LEFT: Earlshall (page 52)

BELOW LEFT: Topiary shaped from an old spreading tree (page 54)

BELOW RIGHT: Batter is important—Barham Manor, Suffolk (page 54)

ABOVE LEFT: Pyramids at
Hill Court, Herefordshire (page 54)

ABOVE RIGHT: Columns at
Hidcote Manor (page 54)

LEFT: Ashby St. Ledgers,
Northamptonshire (page 54)

leaf; but the filth it makes in the walks, by the fall of its flowers in the spring, its husks and fruit in the summer, and its leaves in the beginning of autumn, mightily lessens its merit." Elsewhere, he refers to the bad form it takes when not properly trained, such as the trees in the great walk at the Tuileries, where they have more than "one upright foot" and look like "a Christmas candlestick twisted into several branches".

These, then, are the trees and shrubs used within the precincts of the garden, all in some way trained. Without, there were planted the other forest trees usual in woodland. Even so, compared with even the early nineteenth century the number of kinds was very small. Their importance in the design was immense: they formed the vertical element, a vari-textured frame, set on the tapestry-like floor of the parterres, of scythed grass in the walks, or of calm water to relieve these and add the reflection of these walks. Many were the ornaments: statutary, fountains, belvederes and other pleasure-giving devices.

Some of these, too, were "woodworks". They are delightfully described in a chapter headed "Of Porticos, Bowers, and Cabinets of Arbor-work . . . serving to the Decoration and Embellishment of Gardens".

First, we are warned that the author will discuss one type of structure that demand a royal purse, and so can only be undertaken by princes, ministers of state, and persons of the highest quality. It is that comprising those amazing buildings of lattice-work (treillage) formed from fillets of oak, somewhat more than one inch square, and wrought into checkers six or seven inches square, held together by wire and attached to a framework of stronger timber and iron.* They were designed to conform with the classical orders of architecture and on the most magnificent scale. They could be covered with rose-trees, jasmins, honeysuckles and wild vines for the convenience of shade. But it was the skeletal "columns, pilasters, cornices . . . pedaments, jambs, pannels . . . and other ornaments of architecture" that were the essence of the structure: They were very beautiful and magnificent, raising and improving the natural beauty of gardens extremely.

There were, we read, once buildings of this kind that cost at least twenty thousand crowns—but, alas, the intricate woodwork had decayed and there was nothing but the abundance of iron keeping them up.

These were called artificial arbours. Not surprisingly, most people—even princes—became out of conceit with them. They were replaced by natural arbours formed only by the branches of trees "artfully interwoven and sustain'd by strong lattice-work, hoops, poles, etc., which make galleries, porticos, halls, and green vistas, naturally covered. These arbours are planted with female elms,* or Dutch lime-trees, with hornbeam to fill up the lower part; these sorts of trees easily

* I cannot trace a reference to this so-called "female elm" in any other contemporary author.

yielding, and, by the great quantity of their small boughs, forming a very thick brush-wood. You should observe, above all things, never to bend these trees till the second or third year after they are planted, lest, in so doing, you disturb their roots too much, and hinder them from striking firmly into the earth."

There is no mention of yews or evergreens here, but in fact they are referred to elsewhere for use in comparable structures such as halls and amphitheatres.

SOME EXAMPLES

The period of these British gardens designed in the grand French manner covers, say, the years between the Restoration of 1660 and the time when Charles Bridgeman took charge of the royal gardens in 1728—that Bridgeman who, according to Horace Walpole, introduced the use of the ha ha to extend the garden into the surrounding landscape.

It was a great period of architecture—including, for example, the works of Talman, Vanburgh and Wren. Many houses of this time remain, but for reasons of fashion explained in the next chapter all but a few of the gardens in which they are set no longer exist. Neither or very rarely do their topiary nor their hedges, not even when of long-lasting yew—examples of which a century and more older than this still survive in churchyards.

Certainly some of the oldest topiary still existing is at Levens Hall in Westmorland. The topiary garden (and the fine avenues—in the old straight style which was soon to go out of fashion) were designed by a certain Monsieur Beaumont who had been gardener to James II, but later went north and worked for Sir James Graham after that King gave war to William and Mary. The plan of the impressive topiary garden is, apparently, little changed, and there are many fine specimens still remaining. In about 1808, however, the gardener, Mr Forbes, "repaired the ravages which the vogue for the romantic had made at the end of the eighteenth century". It was, presumably, he who in the operation introduced the striking specimens of golden-leaved yew which were not known in Beaumont's day. The parterre-like beds in this garden, though attractive, are bedded out for summer in a nineteenth-century style with plants quite unknown until long after it was made. Curiously, though for a long period it must have been quite outstanding, I can trace no mention of it until a description in *The Gardener's Chronicle* of 1874 (surprisingly it is not, for instance, referred to in Loudon's *Arboretum et Fruticetum Britannicum* of 1838). This was summarized in Veitch's *Manual of Coniferae* with the comment that it is an example where "the topiary foible of our horticultural predecessors is still maintained in all its quaint antagonism to Nature". The illustrated description refers to woodcuts "of some of the most remarkable groups which include figures of the British Lion; Queen Elizabeth and Ladies; the Judge's wig, a number of yews planted in a half circle so as to form an arbour by bringing the branches over the top in a hood or wig-like fashion; and many others. These figures were first formed early in the eighteenth century, so that for upwards of one hundred and eighty years these yews must have had their young growth cut off to keep the figures within the prescribed shape and size, a proof of the astonishing tenacity of life possessed by the yew." In 1901 Sir Reginald Blomfield described it as a deliberate copy of a Dutch model and "a little childish". As it is today, it certainly does not much resemble anything in the style of Le Nôtre, under whom Beaumont is said to have worked.

Elaborate "set pieces" of topiary appear, however, to have been uncommon and individual. Celia Fiennes, during her travels at the end of the seventeenth century, for example, notes that at Woburn some of the trees were "kept cut in works and the shapes of several beasts". More usually, as at Durdans, there were trees "cut piramidy some suger loafe or rather like a mushroom-top". At Fetcham Park there were grass walks set with dwarf greens. At Warwick Castle fine, large gardens had "good gravell and grass walks, squares of dwarf trees of all sorts . . ." It was these minor, simple works of topiary that were so abundant and such a feature of the formal gardens. Their prodigious use can be seen in Knyff drawings; contemporary plans and perspectives are often confirmed by Miss Fiennes and other descriptions. In the design for a small garden for Marshall Tallard at Nottingham* designed by London and Wise, there are marked 40 "pyramids". In Kirkland's survey of the gardens of Melbourne Hall made in 1722,† when the garden had been finished, in the then elaborate garden lying between the house and the end of the present formal pond, there are about 120. All these have now disappeared. Indeed, such carefully clipped trees have been long removed from all gardens, with, I suggest, one most interesting exception. The terraced gardens at Powis Castle, Montgomeryshire, are among the finest in the British Isles. They were built at the end of the seventeenth or very early in the eighteenth century, possibly to the design of William Winde, who certainly worked for the Powis family. Today, these terraces are dominated by huge, neatly clipped yews. In a drawing of 1740 the yews are small, the small pyramids of the day. Their effect now is magnificent and spectacular. What the designer of the garden would think of them as they now are is an interesting question.

Returning to Melbourne, that lovely garden in green, whose main lines are much as they were when Henry Wise completed it (though the elaborate parterres, really essential to ornament what are now lawns in front of the house have gone),

---

* Reproduced in the present author's *A History of British Gardening* (Spring Books 1969).

† Reproduced in *English Gardens and Landscapes,* Christopher Hussey (Country Life 1967).

there is a remarkable feature. It is one of those "natural arbours" to give a "green vista, naturally covered". It is a sombre yew tunnel at whose remote end a fountain plays in the bright light. And the "strong lattice work, hoops, poles, etc.", were, according to an account book of 1726, then being repaired. Incidentally, "The Right Honourable Thomas Coke Esq., Vice Chamberlain", who made this garden, was a subscriber to James's book.

A famous garden of columnar clipped yews is in the National Trust's property at Packwood House, Warwickshire. The house is clearly much earlier than the garden. The topiary seems first to have been brought to general notice by Sir Reginald Blomfield in 1892:* "the most remarkable instance still exists at Packwood . . . where the Sermon on the Mount is literally represented in clipped yews. At the entrance to the 'mount' at the end of the garden, stand four tall yews 20 feet high for the four evangelists, and six on either side for the twelve apostles. At the top of the mount is an arbour formed in a great yew tree called the 'pinnacle of the temple', which was also supposed to represent Christ on the Mount overlooking the evangelists, apostles, and the multitude below; at least, this account of it was given by the gardener, who was pleaching the pinnacle of the temple."

Blomfield, the only authority for a story which has now become established as fact, was clearly a little sceptical about it. He would have been even more so had he seen an aerial photograph of the garden which shows the yews to form a pattern of pyramids marking a typical Restoration garden design; indeed, such pyramids are seen on the lawn immediately in front of the house in a drawing of about 1756. However, the late Christopher Hussey thought that there might well be such a symbolic connotation in the design.†

Another remarkable example of topiary can be seen at Rous Lench Court in Worcestershire. There seems no doubt that part of this, particularly the arbour at its centre, is of great age—one presumes Restoration. It was repaired and, apparently, added to in late Victorian times by the then owner, the Rev. Chafy Chafy. The result is one of the finest pieces of topiary in England, massive in design and quite devoid of eccentricity.

There are, no doubt, here and there other examples of topiary and arbours of the kind fashionable in the days of London and Wise, but surely not many. Does the remarkable yew-covered promenade at Old Colwall in Herefordshire qualify? Traditionally, it does, but there is no confirming evidence.

Scotland is famed more for its remarkable old hedges than decorative topiary. The rather ornamental yew hedges planted in 1702 at Crathes Castle must, however, be mentioned.

* When collecting material for his book (see Appendix II).
† See H. Avray Tipping, *English Gardens,* and Taylor's description of Wilton on p. 27.

CHAPTER 4

Nature and Destruction

At the very end of the seventeenth century there took place—or perhaps one should say there were the first muttered plottings concerning—a violent revolution in the whole attitude of man, and the Englishman in particular, towards the theory and practice of gardening. At that time the views of the period of Le Nôtre, shortly to be translated into English by James, were generally accepted as being the true and only principles of gardening. They held that man dominated and forced nature and natural forms into a rigid, highly artificial mould. London (who died in 1713) and Wise (who lived on until 1738, designing the great and highly formalized garden at Blenheim after his partner's death) were still producing huge quantities of clipped "greens" at Brompton. Yet the revolutionary murmurs had broken out loud when Joseph Addison wrote in his *Remarks on Several Parts of Italy in the Years 1701, 1702, 1703*: "I have not seen any garden in Italy worth taking notice of. The Italians fall as short of the French in this particular, as they excel them in their palaces. It must, however, be said to the honour of the Italians, that the French took from them the first plans of their gardens, as well as of their waterworks; so that the surpassing of them at present is to be attributed to their riches rather than the excellence of their taste."

So much for the writings of one Pliny and the historic garden-making of another. Yet even after Addison visited Italy we have plenty of evidence proving the extraordinary vogue for topiary. Peter Collinson, the Quaker naturalist and introducer of plants, particularly from North America, described the small gardens of his relatives at Peckham which during the last years of the reign of Queen Anne were remarkable for their fine cut "greens". He often went out with them to buy yews. clipped into the shapes of "birds, dogs, men, ships, etc." Not only were they and other evergreens clipped, but at about the same time the Earl of Haddington wrote of the elm trees near London, "this tree grows in great plenty, and the custom there is to cut off all the side branches close by the bole of the tree, and only leave a small head, so that in the winter they look in a manner like a very tall hedge, and in the spring are as bare as maypoles, except the small head".

The story of the revolt against formality in garden design which meant the exclusion of topiary has early origins and cannot be discussed here. There were hints of it even two centuries before the birth of Christ in the writings of Cato:

> Who is there . . . that, looking at these natural falls, and these two rivers, which form so fine a contrast, would not learn to despise our pompous follies, and laugh at artificial Niles, and seas in marble; for, as in our late argument you referred all to Nature, so more especially in things which relate to the imagination, is she our sovereign mistress.

The most prominent publicists of the new movement were Joseph Addison, already mentioned, about whose own activities as a gardener—if any—nothing is known, and Alexander Pope whose enthusiasm for practical gardening is indicated again and again in his correspondence.

Addison's most violent attack was published in *The Spectator* in 1712:

> Writers who have given us an account of China* tell us the inhabitants of that country laugh at the plantations of our Europeans, which are laid out by the rule and line; because they say, any one may place trees in equal rows and uniform figures.
>
> They choose rather to shew a genius in works of this nature, and therefore always conceal the art by which they direct themselves. They have a word,† it seems in their language, by which they express the particular beauty of a plantation, that thus strikes the imagination at first sight, without discovering what it is, that has so agreeable an effect.
>
> Our British gardeners, on the contrary, instead of humouring nature, love to deviate from it as much as possible. Our trees rise in cones, globes and pyramids. We see the marks of the scissors upon every plant and bush. I do not know whether I am singular in my opinion, but for my own part, I would rather look upon a tree in all its luxuriancy and diffusion and branches, than when it is thus cut and trimmed into a mathematical figure: and cannot but fancy that an orchard in flower looks infinitely more delightful, than all the little labyrinths of the most finished parterre. But as our great modellers of gardens have their magazines of plants to dispose, it is very natural for them to tear up all the beautiful plantations, and contrive a plan that may most turn to their own profit, in taking off their evergreens, and the like movable plants, with which their shops are plentifully stocked.

A year later Alexander Pope in *The Guardian* wrote his famous piece of knock-about comedy:

* Sir William Temple in *Upon the Gardens of Epicurus* (1685).
† The word used by Temple was *sharawadgi*—apparently of Japanese, not Chinese origin.

How contrary to the simplicity of Homer (he was referring to the *Odyssey*) is the modern practice of gardening! We seem to make it our study to recede from nature, not only in the various tonsure of greens into the most regular and formal shape, but even in monstrous attempts beyond the reach of the art itself: we run into sculpture and are yet better pleased to have our trees in the most awkward figures of men and animals, than in the most regular of their own . . . (This is an interesting and important point made by Pope.)

A citizen is no sooner proprietor of a couple of yews, but he entertains thoughts of erecting them into giants, like those of Guildhall. I know an eminent cook, who beautified his country seat with a coronation-dinner in greens, where you see the champion flourishing on horseback at one end of the table, and the Queen in perpetual youth at the other.

For the benefit of all my loving countrymen of this curious taste, I shall here publish a catalogue of greens to be disposed of by an eminent town-gardener, who has lately applied to me upon this head. He represents that for the advancement of a politer sort of ornament in the villas and gardens adjacent to this great city, and in order to distinguish those places from the mere barbarous countries of gross nature, the world stands much in need of a virtuoso gardener, who has a turn to sculpture, and is thereby capable of improving upon the ancients in the imagery of evergreens. I proceed to this catalogue:

Adam and Eve in yew; Adam a little shattered by the fall of the tree of Knowledge in the great storm; Eve and the serpent very flourishing.

Noah's Ark in holly, the ribs a little damaged for want of water.

The tower of Babel not yet finished.

St George in box; his arm scarce long enough, but will be in a condition to stick the dragon by next April.

A green dragon of the same, with a tail of ground-ivy for the present.

N.B. Those two are not to be sold separately.

Edward the Black Prince in Cypress . . .

A Queen Elizabeth in Phillyrea, a little inclining to the Green sickness, but full of growth . . .

An old Maid of Honour in wormwood.*

A topping Ben Jonson in Laurel.

Divers eminent modern poets in bays, somewhat blighted, to be disposed of a pennyworth . . .

Pope surely could have been mocked in turn for the important feature of his garden to which he was devoted:

At the Entrance of the Grotto, next the Garden, are various sorts of Stones thrown promiscuously together, in imitation of an old Ruine; some full of Holes, others like

* *Artemisia absinthium.*

Honey-combes, which came from *Ralph Allen's*, Esq; at *Widcomb* near *Bath*; Several fine Fossils and Snake-stones, with petrified Wood, and Moss in various Shapes, from the petrifying Spring at *Nasborough* in *Yorkshire*, by the Reverend Doctor *Key*. Fine Verd Antique from *Egypt*, with several sorts of *Italian* sparry Marble of diverse Colours. Amethysts, several Clumps of different Forms, with some fine Pieces of White Spar, from her Grace the Duchess of *Cleveland* at *Rabey*-Castle in *Westmorland*. Some fine Pieces of *German* Spar intermixt with Yellow Mundic, with Moss, and some *English Pebbles*. In the Center is a fine Spring.

If we are a little unkind to one of England's greatest poets and a most ardent and intelligent practical gardener, it is to get a something of our own back on that group of literary persons whose prejudices destroyed the carefully designed formal settings of our seventeenth-century houses, an example of vandalism comparable with those we commit today.

In Scotland, the new ideas were not readily accepted. That great tree planter the sixth Earl of Haddington writing of his experiences at Tyninghame in about 1732–5 has this:

The yew, if not kept down by formal clipping, arrives to great beauty and value; but it requires many years, besides care in the management, to bring them to a tolerable size; and therefore few care to plant them, since for these fifty years past, the clipping, and, I think, the spoiling of them, has been in practice. I have now cut all the feathering off my yews, and reduced them to single stems; how they will succeed I cannot tell, but I shall never try to put any evergreen in any shape but its own, unless in a hedge.

As to the holly, when it is trained up to a tree, it is a very beautiful plant; but is likewise spoiled by clipping. I have observed that wherever there is a large yew or hollytree, everyone is liberal in their praises; but, because clipping them is so much in fashion, none has courage enough to plant them as trees, though I not only do it, but have reduced my pyramids, and hope to bring them to their natural shapes.

I intend to try the training of the cherry-bay and the laurel, to trees; and I have some young ones that give me great hopes of success. There are besides, the sweet-bay, phylera and alaternus; these I intend to raise to as great height as I can. I have none of the large box here, but I intend to get some. We have the laurustinus and arbutus, which are only bushes here; and a few larch, which I believe may be worth while to propagate; I neither like the Swedish nor common juniper, far less the Savine. I shall now speak a little of

A WILDERNESS

As it is only raised for shade and ornament, and is laid out in what figure the owner pleases, there can be no rule given: They have not been long introduced into this country, and the way they were first laid out was, they first pitched on a center with

ABOVE: Dignity at Blickling (page 54)

BELOW: Magnificence at Powis Castle (page 54)

Alton Towers—the
yew arcade (page 54)

Topiary framing
a gate (page 54)

straight views from it, terminating in as fine a prospect as could be had; then were there serpentine works that run through the whole, hedged like the straight walks, and the angles planted with variety of different trees; though now they are weary of the hedges. But people who make it their business to lay out ground for gentlemen, are, in my opinion, very unfit for it, for they are too formal and stiff; besides, they make everything so bushy that they croud the ground too much. Were I to plant a wilderness, there should be nothing in it but evergreens trained up as much to trees as I could, flowering trees and them that have fine blossoms, with a kind of willow, that has a bark of bright yellow, when everything looks withered.*

While talking of Tyninghame, it is interesting to recall that when Joseph Sabine, secretary of the Horticultural Society of London, visited the estate in 1825 he remarked on the by now huge holly hedges that were planted by the Earl in 1712.

Soon, Lancelot "Capability" Brown, inspired by William Kent, began his massive destruction of the formal gardens and their great traditions.

* Presumably *Salix alba* 'Vitellina', a golden-twigged form of this common white willow known to Linnaeus.

CHAPTER 5

War Again

NATURE IN DEFEAT

While Humphry Repton, "Capability" Brown's successor, was still alive, a reaction set in against their style. They had brought into being many countryside, park-like landscapes (today in their turn disappearing). Brown is credited with 170, Repton 187.* Their professional and particularly amateur imitators were concerned with many more.

The leader of this movement for a return to the traditional style, though very critical of the absurdities of extreme formality, was the Herefordshire squire, Uvedale Price. He launched his vitriolic attack on Brown and his school in *An Essay on the Picturesque* in 1794, a remarkably subtle and learned book in which lie the origins of the modern landscape garden with its picturesque effects and extensive use of exotic trees, shrubs and plants.

Price, as a young man and one of the many amateurs who blindly followed the fashion of Brown, had destroyed his old Herefordshire garden. This he came to regret. Referring to his condemnation of Brown and his school, he wrote:

> I may perhaps have spoken more feelingly on this subject, from having done myself what I so condemn in others,—destroyed an old fashioned garden. It was not indeed in the high style of those I have described,† but it had many of the same circumstances, and had their effect. As I have long since perceived the advantage which I could have made of them, and how much I could have added to that effect; how well I could in parts have mixed the modern style, and have altered and concealed many of the stiff and glaring formalities, I have long regretted its destruction. I destroyed it, not from disliking it; on the contrary, it was a sacrifice I made against my own sensations, to the prevailing opinion. I doomed it and all its embellishments, with which I had formed such an early connection to sudden and total destruction; probably much upon the same

* H. C. Prince, *Parkland in the English landscape*, Amateur Historian, III.
† Such as the Villa Negroni.

idea, as many a man of careless, unreflecting, good nature, thought it his duty to vote for demolishing towns, provinces, and their inhabitants, in America: like me (but now different the scale and the interest!) they chose to admit it as a principle, that whatever obstructed the prevailing *system*, must be all thrown down—all laid prostrate: no medium, no conciliatory methods tried, but that whatever might follow, destruction must precede.

I remember, that even this garden (so infinitely inferior to those of Italy) had an air of decoration, and of gaiety, arising from that decoration,—*un air paré*—a distinction from mere unimbellished nature, which, whatever the advocates for extreme simplicity may allege, is surely essential to an ornamental garden: all beauties of undulating ground, of shrubs and of verdure, are to be in places where no art has ever been employed, and consequently cannot bestow a distinction which they do not possess, for they must themselves in some respects be considered as unimbellished nature.

He goes on to delight in terraces with their varied aspects, in fruit trees, shrubs and statues disposed with some formality, and the desirability (so well understood by our ancestors) of walled apartments giving an appearance of seclusion and safety.

Today, it is difficult to realize the extent to which these things had been erased from gardens—and we should heed his warning of following fashionable changes, now disguised under (to those who are practical gardeners) such meaningless phrases as labour saving, with the concomitant destruction, noises and smells of expensive machinery. Nor should we be carried away by the excesses of modern "plantsmanship".

Alas, nowhere in his writings (so far as I can trace) does Price refer to topiary. Of the *outré* examples such as Levens Hall this man of great learning, taste and sensibility would certainly have disapproved. But he refers so repeatedly to his delight in and approval of architectural and other ornaments and embellishments that he must have approved of the rigidly clipped trees and hedges, and of the even more closely sheared shrubs bordering parterres, which formed a singularly important element in their design from the days of Pliny onwards.

The strictures of Pope and Addison, combined with the Englishman's alleged love of nature, lingered on. In Loudon's great *Encyclopaedia of Gardening*, 1827 edition (which was reprinted at least four times), there appears to be no reference to topiary. But we have, rather patronizingly, "*Vegetable sculptures* are very appropriate in parterres and other scenes in the ancient style. That they may be executed with correctness and without loss of time, the skeleton should be formed of wire,* within which all the shoots, and when the form is filled up with vegetation, the

* Wire netting was not then in use.

gardener has only to clip the protruding shoots. Groups of figures of different colours may be very curiously executed by using different colored greens. In the garden of the convent of the Madre de Dio, near Savonna, is a group representing the flight of Joseph into Egypt, in yellow box, variegated holly, myrtle, cypress, laurel and rosemary. The attending priest told us these plants completed their forms in three years."

Perhaps a hint of relaxation from Pope's "Nature"!

Further on, we have his rather ambivalent "*Pruning for ornament or beauty* must be guided in its operations by what that beauty is. If it is the beauty of art, the tree may require to be cut or clipped into the shape of animals; or inanimate natural objects, as mounds of earth, mushrooms; or geometric forms, triangles, globes, cones; or walks, columns, arcades, vases, arbors, temples, theatres or other architectural or sculptural compositions."

Even more convincing evidence of the continued decline, or at least lack of development, is found in Loudon's great *Arboretum et Fruiticetum Britannicum* of 1838, in statements concerning certain shrubs, as for example to *Spiraea hypericifolia* that "it will bear the shears, which were formerly applied to it, to shape into artificial forms, when topiary work was fashionable".

Another celebrated *Dictionary of Gardening*, G. W. Johnson's, first published in 1846 and subsequently in revised editions, makes no mention of the craft.

However, by then the exuberance of Victorian arboriculture and horticulture was developing and including topiary in its surge.

For a summary of the state of affairs there is *A Manual of the Coniferae* published in 1881 by James Veitch and Son of Chelsea, the anonymous author being Adolphus H. Kent.

The point is made, as it was in other publications, that topiary declined because the introduction of exotic hardy evergreen trees became more widespread, and supplied a more natural and pleasing variety than the uncouth figures which one kind of tree was made to take, but into which nature never intended it to grow. This is a very dubious claim, far more closely connected with taste and fashion than arboriculture.

In comparison with Levens, indeed, Kent wrote:

Not less striking but more modern, and, if we may use the expression, more rational, is the topiary work of Elvaston Castle, near Derby, the seat of the Earl of Harrington.* A large portion of this consists of ornamental hedges of the common yew, either dividing parts of the grounds from each other, or enclosing spaces devoted to special subjects; and of single specimens, both of the common yew and its golden variety, cut

* Now a country park. The Earl is commemorated by *Cephalotaxus harringtonia*, the odd "cows-tail" pine, introduced from Japan in 1830.

The topiary sundial, Ascott (page 55)

The fountain garden, Ascott (page 55)

Cake-stand, St. Fagan's Castle (page 55)

Cake-stand with handle, Ashperton, Herefordshire (page 55)

Parterre in the French manner, Oxburgh Hall (page 57)

into conical pyramids of uniform size and height, and of such there are upwards of one thousand. There are comparatively few representations of birds and animals; the bolder work represents the bastions of a Norman castle, archways, alcoves, arbours, etc. The great extent of the topiary work is calculated to excite surprise rather than admiration, at the same time its extreme formality is greatly relieved by the noble conifers of the fir and pine tribe which have been planted beside and around it with no sparing hand, and by the beautiful view afforded by the river Derwent, in its winding course through the grounds.

Kent does not seem to have appreciated the extent of the revival of topiary in the British Isles. Many more fine examples date from before and just after this period than those of which Kent was aware. The superb and dignified banks of topiary at Sudeley Castle, with parterre-like beds between them, were created in the eighteen-forties. The numerous individual and delightfully fantastic and peculiar oddities that lie beside the lovely Tudor house of Compton Wynyates, sunk in its deep hollow among the Warwickshire hills, was a product of the eighteen-nineties.

Kent concludes by describing the kind of topiary that we all know so well today, which has been common for centuries and is still being created. It is always the work of ordinary gardeners working with enthusiasm, patience and ingenuity and keeping alive, in spite of the changing fashions brought about by those often tiresome aestheticians of garden design, a tradition that is many centuries old: "Throughout the counties of Kent and Sussex, and also many other parts of England, chiefly in the gardens of old farm houses and wayside inns, yet may be seen an ancient yew* clipped into the figure of a bird or quadruped; the peacock appearing to have been popular with the yeomanry, and the fox and greyhound with innkeepers." Today, there is much greater variety of subject—such as the horse and jockey outside a Herefordshire cottage.

Kent quotes Tennyson's *Enoch Arden*:

> *The climbing street, the mill, the leafy lane,*
> *The peacock yew tree, and the lonely Hall . . .*

THE BATTLE REVIVED

The vogue for formality with its parterres and topiary had, indeed, returned long before the *Manual of Coniferae* was published. In 1834 Loudon's *Gardener's Magazine* had published a design by Lewis Kennedy laid out at Woolmers,

* Or, indeed, many a one not so ancient!

Hertfordshire, some years before which was the type then coming into fashion and which was to dominate the Victorian garden. In the eighteenth century the design itself was paramount. In the nineteenth, design was secondary to horticulture, and as in this instance was, to say the least, pedestrian. The gravel walks were framed in box, except up against the grass beds which formed an inner and outer circle and which was dotted with shrubs mixed with exotic plants taken from the greenhouse and plunged into their pots for the summer season. The shaded beds were filled with roses or dahlias, or roses mixed with dahlias. We have, therefore, a foretaste of the new and increasingly popular practice of "bedding out", the use of tender plants giving a display only during summer, the beds being empty and lifeless during much of the year.

A much more interesting variant on the parterre theme was described by Loudon in 1838. It was at Woburn—for centuries famed for its remarkable gardens— and was designed for and planted entirely with hardy heaths, which then as now were very fashionable. It was called a "symmetrical ericetum", considerable effects being attained by the carefully used varying heights of the different kinds.

Among the exponents of the "architectural style", as it was now called, was W. A. Nesfield, a retired soldier who began designing gardens in about 1840 and continued for some forty years. For the Horticultural Society's Gardens at Kensington in 1861, for example, he laid out designs of the rose, thistle, shamrock and leek, using only box with various minerals. He sometimes worked on gardens designed by his predecessors such as Brown and Repton, devising formal schemes around the house. Remains of his work in an Italianate manner are still to be seen in several places.*

The greatest exponent of this Italian style, and one who worked on the grandest scale, was Sir Charles Barry. His huge architectural schemes at Shrubland Park in Suffolk and Trentham Park in Staffordshire remain, but have been emasculated by the removal of the parterres. There were many other gardens with less magnificent structural features, designed in a geometrical manner descending somewhat from Italian or French models, but tricked out in all the nineteenth-century glory of floriculture, which have now, under the pressure of "good taste" (or perhaps fashion) and more realistically the economic situation, disappeared. A remarkable example is Drummond Castle in Perthshire. Today, it seems like an anachronism— very much as it was in 1883, when William Robinson used it as an example to launch a further attack on formality in garden design: "One of those wonderful displays of 'bedding out' in its cruder forms, which attains its greatest 'glory' near large Scottish houses. Plants in squares, repeated by hundreds and thousands walks from which all interest is taken by the planting on each side being of exactly

---

* His brother-in-law was the architect Anthony Salvin, with whom he often worked.

the same pattern." If is an echo of Pope's frequently quoted castigation of our great formal gardens:

Grove nods at grove, each alley has a brother,
And half the platform just reflects the other.

Robinson, rumbustious, immensely influential and a great plantsman, was somewhat intemperate. He objected to the gardens at Versailles, "a vast, graceless and inert design"; "the far from beautiful garden at Caserta"; "the deplorable result of trying to adapt Italian modes to English gardens executed by Sir Charles Barry", while Paxton's Crystal Palace gardens he considered the "greatest modern example of the waste of enormous means in making hideous a fine piece of ground". Inevitably his contempt for parterres was great, and of topiary: ". . . apart from the ugliness of the cocked-hat tree and other pantomimic trees, the want of life and change in a garden made up of such trees, one would think, should open the eyes of anyone to its drawbacks as in it there is none of the joys of spring's life, or summer's crown of flowers, or winter's rest."

Robinson considered that the garden was made for hardy plants, not plants for the garden. The architect, even the artist, should keep out. Fortunately, he became associated with Miss Gertrude Jekyll, who was a consummate example of the second, who was in turn closely associated with Sir Edwin Lutyens, the last of our great architects before the utterly inhuman Teutonic and French functionalism took charge.

Fortunately, too, Robinson was answered by two architects. Reginald Blomfield first produced *The Formal Garden in England* as a challenge to him in 1892. A great authority on renaissance architecture, but not perhaps himself a first-rate architect, this book was the first scholarly study of the subject to be published in this country and was embellished with exquisite drawings by Inigo Thomas, in addition to reproductions of old prints. It quite correctly placed—in a perfect garden—the designer before the gardener, as the architect comes before the builder. It annoyed Robinson, who was not, I think, capable of appreciating the subtleties of architecture and architectural decoration as was Miss Jekyll, as is shown by her magnificent *Garden Ornaments* of 1918 with many splendid examples illustrated.,

Blomfield was concerned only with the formal gardens of the past. A far more interesting opponent of Robinson was the architect J. D. Sedding, who published his *Garden Craft Old and New* in 1891. He was a prominent member of the Art Workers Guild, with friends such as Lethaby, Burne-Jones and Walter Crane. His book is fortunately largely concerned with the "new"—his own ideas. The drawings show some interesting new shapes—tending to *art nouveau*.

Another important and fascinating study of formality with, as the reader of his son Osbert's writings will be entertainingly aware, a strong leaning towards Italy, was Sir George Sitwell's *On the Making of Gardens*, published in 1909.

The consequence was that, in spite of Robinson's aggressive attitude towards the "tonsile arts", the end of the nineteenth and the early twentieth centuries saw some finely designed topiary executed on the grand scale, usually designed by architects with an understanding of the material. A notable example is at Earlshall, Fife, the work of Sir Robert Lorimer in about 1895.

The years 1914–18 shattered all previous standards of gardening, as of all other civilized activities, on the grand scale; 1939 finally eclipsed them, making "labour saving" the inescapable and savagely efficient tyrant of the garden designer.

Nevertheless, the first quarter of the present century ended with Nathaniel Lloyd's *Garden Craftsmanship in Yew and Box* (1925), so far as I know the first consequential practical study of the subject. It was largely exemplified by his own work at Great Dixter in Sussex. With its many illustrations, it is just as valuable today, when we are forced to operate on a miniscule scale, as when it was published.

And the year 1907 saw the beginning of Hidcote Manor Garden in Gloucestershire by Major Lawrence Johnstone. The imagination used in the use of the principal elements of formal design, and particularly of hedges and topiary, remains unsurpassed, and has proved a powerful influence on the smaller gardens in which great care and attention has been given to design, such as Sissinghurst Castle and many others.

CHAPTER 6

Today

TOPIARY

There are now many more examples of topiary in the category that includes "satyrs, whales, and half-man horses" in small roadside country gardens, outside inns and by farm-houses found standing in isolation, than there are large groups of these fanciful oddities in the gardens of the great, whence many have been reduced on account of the pressure of economics or disappeared along with the gardens that surrounded them. A few examples of this fanciful, even absurd topiary are, however, still to be found.

How, one may ask, were these often elaborate artificialities formed? The first thing to remember is that, at least for the most part, they were (and are) not raised and shaped by experts, but by the innkeeper or cottager, who has usually invented the design. A well-fed young yew remains leafy down to its base, and in addition has a main leader which will grow at perhaps 30 cm a year with two or three subsidiary leaders. One or more of these can be selected when the tree is large enough and tied to a framework at an angle to its normal growth to form the main structure: this, in due course, will branch and can be cut into the required shape. Light bamboo can be used for the frame. The shoots can be tied with thick tarred string, not too tightly, which must be removed if it gets tight and, if necessary, replaced. The tie must never strangle the shoot.

It is, of course, practically impossible to do much in the way of beginning an elaborate piece of topiary work with trees of the small size usually purchased to start a hedge. Plants must be grown on until there is enough growth and long enough shoots to work with. Probably many, if not most, of the ornate sculptures were begun when the trees were quite sizeable, remembering the fact that even an old yew can be cut back hard to its very skeleton and break into leaf and incipient shoots all along the bare wood. This savage pruning should be done in spring, after the danger of severe frost, which can scorch the young growth badly before it has become seasoned and hardy. The example shown, facing page 36, was formed from an old spreading tree touching the roof of the cottage.

Of the simpler shapes, most effective is the present-day garden in the tetrahedron—the "pyramid" of the eighteenth century. It has four sides sloping inwards from a broad rectangular base, the top being flattened. The sides are flat and straight, or can be slightly curved; the angle of the slope can be varied to suit the situation. A good example is seen at Hill Court, Herefordshire, used in a simplified version of a Victorian garden. The same shape can be used, broader-based and lower at the termination of a hedge. The top can be brought to a blunt point.

In these angular, flat-surfaced shapes regularity is essential; batter (the slope from the ground inwards towards the top) is an important feature emulating in a rigid way natural growth, narrowing as it exhausts strength as it thrusts upwards. A most attractive effect, used in moderation, can be achieved by the reverse—that is, the top heavy and sloping in to the base. A good example of this is at Ashby St Ledgers, amplified by its reflection in calm water: this was, I believe, the work of Lutyens. Another good instance is in the parterre around Castle Howard. From the practical point of view, however, this is not ideal,

These slopes and levels, as Nathaniel Lloyd wrote, are less easy to cut with the accuracy essential to them than are curved surfaces. If the eye cannot cope, a light frame forming a template for the section and a taut line help.

The cone, broad-based, round-topped—even globular—is a frequent and valued motif. Tall, narrow, blunt-topped and placed in a rigid line as a column, it forms a spectacular boundary at the side of one of the many small side gardens at Hidcote.

Another columnar and dignified effect is attained by repeated use of the narrow cone on a circular base. Great use of this is made, along with other substantial shapes, in the formal garden in front of the house at Blickling.

These are units used repetitively in a design.

Another frequent and effective use of the yew's sombre green is a solitary one, either as a frame for some object or a restriction to enclose a view. Thus, in the absence of anything else significant, a balanced, plain block of yew not infrequently forms an arch over a gate, as may be seen (in this case, one suspects, a collector's trophy) at Daneway House in Gloucestershire. But something similar may often be seen elsewhere, often elaborated and giving dignity and character to an otherwise insignificant entrance. Yew helps to make a magnificent setting for a magnificent and apparently little-used gate at Powis Castle used as a feature in the design.

At Alton Towers, one of the finest nineteenth-century gardens in England, but surprisingly little known outside the industrial north, there is a single form of arch used in some places as an individual feature, but more strikingly in a whole series to form an arcade.

The number and variety of rose gardens and other features enclosed within yew walls and disclosed through a well-placed opening are many. But, I think uniquely in what might be called a close walk of yews at Hill Court in Herefordshire. As one progresses down it, on one side are niches cut for statuary, and on the other apertures giving peepshow-like views of the massive ruin of Goodrich Castle on its rock above the River Wye—perhaps an early Victorian, and most effective, picturesque conceit.

A complete contrast and a most original design in a comparatively modern garden where topiary in every form is lavishly used is at Ascott in Buckinghamshire. Here is a most ingenious feature on the border of the garden framing a circular fountain pool and leading on to a wide vista of the countryside out into Bedfordshire.

This National Trust garden also gives us a very good, if exceptional, example of that other type of topiary, the solitary feature, in the form of a topiary clock. No one could complain, as did writers on many early examples such as Levens, that it is "uncouth". Another good and distinctive design for a solitary eye-catching feature which is not uncommon has, so far as I can find, no particular name. It somewhat resembles those racks, long out of fashion, which carried a series of plates bearing elaborate cakes and bread and butter, thin as wafers, which were a necessary adjunct to the flimsy, polite tea table. Crudely described, it is a narrow tree cut into a series of discs, decreasing in diameter as they proceed upwards, showing the single stem between each. Nathaniel Lloyd illustrates the formation of something in this style from an existing tree; there is a nice example at St Fagans, and a variation outside a public house at Ashperton, Herefordshire with, presumably, a handle added!

The spiral is another delightful feature whose method of formation is perplexing. In fact, it is quite simple. A young plant is kept to a single shoot which, as it grows, is trained to spiral round a stake. The side shoots are then allowed to grow to give substance, and are kept clipped. There is a good example of this design on a small scale in box at Malcolm House at Batsford in Gloucestershire, near Moreton-in-Marsh. Box can, of course, be used to create small-scale versions of all these designs. Rarely a topiary garden cut entirely in box is encountered. A well-known example is at Chastleton House in the Cotswolds.

Many are the other different shapes into which topiary is cut, of which examples can be seen all over the British Isles. Surprisingly, I have never seen two designs which look quite practicable illustrated, and I think invented by John D. Sedding in his *Garden Craft Old and New* of which sketches are appended. They might be called designs in the *art nouveau* style.

Once a design has come into being, all that remains is the tedious clipping.

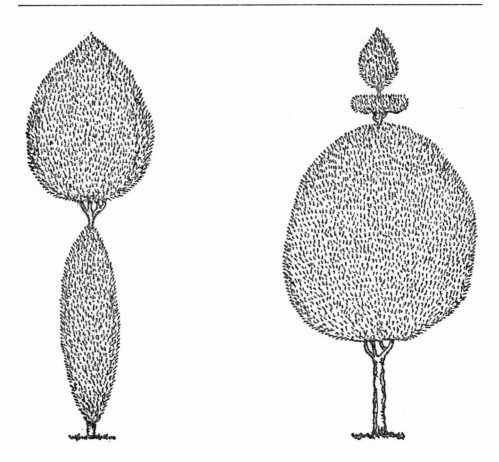

Power-driven clippers are now available in several designs, and are immensely labour saving. Yet on inquiring of those responsible for maintaining some particularly good examples, I have always found that they are not used. The touch of artistry needed can only be obtained by the human hand using shears.

PARTERRES

The parterre, even as it existed in the first part of the present century, is a rare feature in gardens today. The reason is inevitably that of the continual labour needed not only in clipping but weeding. The complexity of the work means that labour-saving devices are of little help. Carpet bedding—still practical in local authority gardens—is perhaps a substitute. This is a purely annual affair, the design being effective only for a season and often as not altered each year: a parterre is a permanent design worked out with great care and thought. This is exemplified by the astonishing example to the south-east of Blenheim Palace created and laid out by the ninth Duke of Marlborough between 1900 and 1910, the designer being Achille Duchêne, brought up in the great French tradition. The later water garden to the south-west of the house also makes use of parterre work. These astonishing achievements, the like of which do not exist in the British Isles, place Vanbrugh's great palace in a setting comparable with, though different from, that designed for it originally by Henry Wise. That masterpiece, of which plans exist, was destroyed by "Capability" Brown when he brought the grass of the park, containing the lake he created out of the little River Glyme, up to the walls of the building. It gives an idea of the catastrophic change that the "Naturalistic" movement of Addison and Pope brought about in destroying the setting that was so carefully conceived.

The achievements of Blenheim can only be appreciated by inspection; the scale is such that the camera cannot grasp it. Even so, it does not quite achieve the lightness and almost reckless gaiety of the Continental work as illustrated by d'Argenville, which can still be seen on the Continent. It was still very occasionally caught in Victorian times, as for example by the careful and scholarly Barry at Shrubland Park.

One small example in that gay style that can be seen in England is rather surprisingly and inappropriately in the garden of that huge, red, fifteenth-century gate tower at Oxburgh Hall in Norfolk. It is well worth climbing to its top to look down upon it—as parterres should be looked at. This French design, the origin of which can be traced, was probably added when additional buildings were added in Victorian times.

There is a fine, bold, angular design on either side of the wide lawn at Cliveden in Buckinghamshire, presumable designed by Barry, who built the house in 1851.

Generally speaking, the British parterre, after the mid-Victorian revival, is now more closely related to the old and simpler knot garden. Almost always it is carried out in box, a tradition long established and reinforced by the distinguished and influential James Anderson in *The New Practical Gardener and Modern Horticulturist* of 1871: "All things considered, there is nothing neater, better, or more appropriate for all descriptions of garden edgings than box. Grass edgings, of course, are quite admissible; but where there are designs on gravel, box is undoubtedly much to be preferred. We say so with a full knowledge of encaustic tiles, ornamental ceramic work of all kinds, and even of thrift and heather, both of which make highly ornamental edgings."

Of many possible examples in the traditional style, the box maze at Gayhurst in

Buckinghamshire and part of the considerable and appropriate parterres in the garden of Vanbrugh's magnificent Seaton Delaval Hall in Northumberland may be mentioned.

A very interesting garden is at Pitmedden in Aberdeenshire. Here, the Scottish National Trust in a delightful seventeenth-century setting of walls and buildings has created a box-edged parterre garden partly based on a contemporary design and partly original. The planting of the beds is modern in conception and full of colour. It could be described as an inspired guess at what the original creator of this "Great Garden" would have produced had he had at his disposal the plants we use today.

This attractive garden suggests that, using the many kinds of small shrubs that are now available and will stand clipping, much greater use of their variety of colour, texture and form might be made to design attractive and more or less permanent forms of parterre-style beds which, beyond periodical clipping, would need little attention.

SUBSTITUTES FOR TOPIARY

Since the two great eras of the formal garden—that is, during the seventeenth and mid-nineteenth centuries—a number of naturally erect-growing, columnar conifers have been introduced which are more or less suitable to replace the pyramids once so frequently used. These need little if any clipping.

The best known is the Irish yew, *Taxus baccata* 'Fastigiata'. A singular example of its use is at Dartington Hall in Devonshire, where it is, I think, lightly clipped; here its use is entirely formal. It can be used to delineate a vista in an informal garden such as Daneway House in Gloucestershire. It can in mild districts in time reach 15 m, but this is unusual. It is much more likely to increase in breadth. A pair forms a splendid frame for a vista. The form 'Fastigiata Aurea' is a rich yellow, and slower growing.

There are several kinds of Lawson's cypress which are suitable. Care must be taken in their selection, as some which look ideal when young have branches which later fall apart in heavy snow, and from then on the trees must either be bound up by cord or encircled by green wide-mesh plastic netting. The most reliable is 'Allumii', a dark, slightly glaucous green, which has, however, an arching leader. It will in time—a long time—reach 18 m. The same may be said of 'Erecta' ('Erecta viridis'), which has variants 'Erecta Alba', 'Erecta Aurea' and 'Erecta Filiformis'. The form known as 'Fletcheri' (sold for rockeries!) is a delightful, slow-growing tree with greyish-green, feathery foliage, remaining erect under all conditions. 'Fraseri' is narrowly erect with glaucous branches. 'Pottenii', though popular, should be avoided. A very narrow tree grown at Wisley as 'Stricta' is particularly slender. 'Wissellii' is eventually far too big, but lovely when young, particularly when densely covered with its crimson flowers.

Very good indeed is a slender, glaucous tree that has a variety of names such as *Cupressus arizonica* or *glabra* 'Pyramidalis'.

Juniperus chinensis has narrow forms, erect when young, but seldom remaining so in age.

J. communis hibernica, the Irish juniper, often described as erect and suitable for formal gardens, is to be avoided; it needs regular tying-in and training.

A tree of great promise is *Juniperus* 'Sky Rocket', which is extremely narrow. It is a recent introduction, and whether it will eventually prove satisfactory is not known.

An excellent formal tree is *Thuya occidentalis* 'Fastigiata'. It is persistently rigid, narrow and slow-growing. The foliage is green in summer, bronze in winter.

I think all these and others may be seen and examined, correctly labelled, at both the Bedgebury Pinetum, Goudhurst, and the Royal Horticultural Society's Garden at Wisley.

DECIDUOUS ARBOURS AND WOODWORKS

From very early accounts already quoted it is clear that such deciduous shrubs as hawthorn were cut into fantastic shapes. I do not know of any examples today. On the other hand, we can find examples of "natural arbours formed only by the branches of trees artfully interwoven, and sustained by strong latticework, hoops, poles, etc."

They were, d'Argenville wrote, formed of female elms or Dutch lime trees, with hornbeam to fill the lower part.

Probably the most frequent examples of this practice until recent time was the training of fruit trees at regular intervals over arches above a wide path. The arches were, I think, of iron. The trees were treated as cordons and spur pruned: they were primarily grown for their fruit and usually in the kitchen garden. One rarely sees an example of this type of training, which might well be revived as an ornamental feature.

The best known and a most delightful instance of what might be classified as a green vista is the lime tunnel in front of the orangery at Kensington Palace. The trees are, I think, the common or Dutch lime recommended by d'Argenville. Apart from the fact that it becomes affected by aphides which drip honey-dew, the bushy growths on the stem which make it so undesirable as an avenue tree are in this case no disadvantage. The arched-over trees are pleached, that is the shoots are bent and intertwined. An interesting example of a similar tunnel in its early stages can be seen at St Fagans Castle near Cardiff.

An extraordinary tunnel is in the Zoo at Regent's Park, consisting of weeping ash. In winter the contortions and writhings of its branches make a fascinating design. This is trained on an elaborate iron framework.

What would, I suppose, have been called palisades—straight lines of deciduous trees with pleached branches—are still sometimes seen. Again, there are good examples at St Fagans, both low and tall. At Wallington in Northumberland there is a tall palisade in which only the upper part is trained fan-wise.

A most delightful example of simple pleaching is seen guarding the upper windows of a house facing the street in Wickham Market, Suffolk.

Particularly at Wallington, where the trunk below the fan is bare, the disadvantages of using the common lime (*T. europaea* or *vulgaris*)—the Dutch lime of old authors—is seen. As already mentioned, nothing will prevent it making unsightly bushy growths from the ground and old trees high up in the crown, but particularly on what should be the bare trunk; when pruned off, they grow again with vigour. This defect is almost absent on our native limes, the small-leaved (*Tilia cordata*) and the more vigorous and quicker growing large-leaved (*T. platyphyllos*). This last also has a red-twigged form.

Either of these two limes could be used for a type of "woodwork" whose name I have never seen mentioned by old authors, though its origins are not new. "Stilt hedge" seems to be the term used nowadays. It is in effect a neatly clipped hedge raised some feet above the ground on the bare trunks of the tree used. The individual trees are planted so as to give an effect of a regular series of bare columns supporting an entablature. There is a celebrated example at Hidcote Manor in Gloucestershire in which hornbeam is used: the silver columns support a block of green in summer and copper in winter. Another good example is at Earlshall.

Perhaps we should also include arbours within naturally weeping trees. Their height is regulated by the length of stem on to which the "weeper" is grafted. The best trees for the purpose are the normal weeping ash (*Fraxinus excelsior* 'Pendula') and the Camperdown weeping elm (*Ulmus glabra* 'Camperdownii')—the usual weeping wych elm *U.g.* 'Pendula' is far too spreading.

CHAPTER 7

The Hedge and its Uses

THE HEDGE AND ITS USES

Few countries have their land so interlaced with hedges as the British Isles; they are present and are, or have been until recently, dominant in all agricultural districts except where owing to geological conditions stone walls replace them. There are two reasons for this. First, most of agricultural England was anciently woodland, and provides a natural habitat for woody plants; second, the Enclosure Acts principally in late eighteenth and early nineteenth centuries necessitated the planting of many, many miles of hedgerows to delineate the newly defined boundaries. In the circumstances, although our still densely hedged landscape is comparatively new, though developed from the very early sparse use of hedges, it is not surprising that the hedge in all sorts of sizes, forms and materials plays an immensely important part in the outer and interior boundaries and divisions of our gardens. It has, particularly today, the advantage of long life, and apart from clipping, which can now be carried out quickly by machinery, a much greater and less expensive adaptability to changing circumstances than a wall. Hedges that are centuries old still exist and are satisfactory, whereas contemporary walls would have crumbled away.

Further, while for centuries our garden hedges were formed of our native trees and shrubs (except for a few introduced kinds used from, say, the late sixteenth century onwards for minor hedges and parterres—rosemary being a notable example), we have today a whole series of trees and plants providing a great variety of colour, texture, rate of growth and adaptability to environment. (For example, exotic kinds are far more tolerant of windy, seaside conditions than our natives).

The lists that follow in Appendix I name a selection of trees and shrubs suitable for differing purposes and with a variety of qualities, and details of their cultivation.

But first, it is desirable to make a few general comments on the use of hedges and their management.

Principally, I suppose, their purposes are to define the outer boundary of a garden and often in addition to give shelter and protection. For this purpose our strong-growing natives are best, except under seaside conditions. Holly, occasionally seared in bitter winters, but seldom badly damaged; yew, undesirable as an outer boundary to which stock has access owing to the toxicity of the leaves, particularly when clipped; beech and hornbeam, the traditional staple deciduous plants, remain the most reliable. Further, all these are very hardy and will grow on any soil, however dry—including chalk—excluding that which is badly drained. It is a rule that deciduous trees are more satisfactory than evergreens in smoky, dusty urban conditions. Though holly and yew (and most evergreens) will grow reasonably well under town conditions and are splendid when the new leaves glisten, after the year or two for which they persist their shine goes and they become drab. The normal country hedgerow, with its varied flora, is, of course, excellent for the purpose where it already exists and has developed naturally. It is, I think, impossible to create this with all its glories other than by the hand of time —and this book is, from its very subject, concerned with artifice rather than nature.

One newcomer, an evergreen which shows great promise, is the so-called western red cedar, *Thuya plicata*. It is less sombre than the yew, and without any sinister qualities. It is hardy, stands the shears well, is reasonably quick growing and except in the seedling stage very reliable. How it will compete in terms of real longevity with our natives is not yet known; it is only now being grown here on any wide scale following its introduction as recently as 1853. It will grow on soils with a high lime content if there is a reasonably good rainfall.

Another much more recent newcomer is the Leyland cypress, *Cupressocyparis leylandii*. So far, there seem to be no conditions in which it will not thrive (including chalk soils) and grow vigorously; in fact, its rate of growth (it needs cutting three times a year) may be a liability.

When we come to extreme seaside conditions, we can again cite the Leyland cypress. It owes this toleration to one of its parents, *Cupressus macrocarpa*, once very popular as a hedge but sometimes killed in very severe winters. By the sea, at least in milder districts where extremes of temperature are unusual, its ability to withstand salt-laden winds (it is a native of north-west America swept by Pacific gales) makes it a suitable, quick-growing hedge plant. Also good, but slow growing, is the surprisingly hardy holm oak from the Mediterranean, *Quercus ilex*, another tree used to salty winds.

These are the principal subjects for substantial clipped hedges intended for a long life. Details for their planting and cultivation are given in Appendix I. But one only has to examine old hedges to realize that spacing varies enormously: the closer one plants the quicker does a dense hedge result. When a very strong, broad hedge is required, the plants may be put in two rows, staggered, say ·6 m apart.

As to the size of the plants used, these are generally offered from about ·5 m to ·75 m high or occasionally larger. As in all tree planting, little time is gained in the end by planting large stuff. It is much more important to be sure that the quality is good, with satisfactory roots, and that it is supplied and planted at the right season.

Even more important, the ground must be well prepared. A strip of ground at least 1 m wide must be well dug and plenty of decayed manure, compost or bone-meal worked in. It is important to plant to a line tightly stretched. After planting it is as well to water each plant individually to ensure that it is well settled in, then to mulch it to prevent drying out in early spring and summer. Regular mulches of lawn mowings subsequently help very considerably and discourage weed growth, which should be kept down until the hedge itself chokes it.

Clipping should be done at the appropriate season according to Appendix I. And always, the leading shoot or shoots should not be cut until the required height has been reached, but the sides should be regularly cut back so that the base of the hedge is broader than the top. Again, a line stretched alongside a hedge when clipping it ensures that the sides are parallel—not always easy to accomplish when growth in a young hedge is uneven.

Old hedges will inevitably have taken much out of the ground and they should be fed at intervals with a general fertilizer, the ground having been loosened first so far as possible by forking. Mulches applied when the ground is wet also do good.

These notes apply to all clipped hedges except those which in Appendix I are described as doing best in light soil, while the dwarf hedges used in parterres are normally planted around flower beds in which the soil is well worked.

The other type of hedge now widely used is that in which pruning is only roughly carried out to form a free-growing informal hedge usually with arching and often flowering branches. This should be planted and treated as above without, of course, the same degree of clipping. More care is needed in weeding this type until it is well established, for the spreading growth hides the weeds.

Modern herbicides can of course, be used freely on deciduous hedges when they are out of leaf, but with evergreen hedges they must be used most carefully on the surrounding ground only so that not a single splash falls on the green growth.

Possibly the most tiresome pest to remove from a hedge is bindweed. At the first sign of its appearance the tips of the shoots must be dipped into a suitable selective weed-killer and this course continued until the weed is destroyed.*

* Owing to continued developments and changes in these rather dangerous substances, inquiries should be made as to the most suitable kind available.

On the other hand, it is often quite delightful to grow decorative climbers in hedges. The scarlet flame flower, *Tropaeolum speciosum*, looks extremely well in a sombre yew hedge. Everlasting peas in their several varieties have long been allowed to ramble in hedges, while many small-flowered clematis and such plants as the not always hardy *Eccremocarpus scaber* in its different colour forms will often thrive among the sheltered growth.

The mixed nature of a natural hedge can also be imitated in a sophisticated manner. A good example is at Hidcote Manor, where a hedge of mixed yew, box, holly, beech and hornbeam was called by the late Miss Sackville-West the "harlequin hedge". A simpler mixture is easily managed. In winter, the two greens of yew and holly—one dull, the other shiny—mixed with the reddish glow of the beech is most satisfactory.

The use of the coloured and variegated forms of the usual hedging materials is a little risky and needs care—or is it daring?

But on looking at the many kinds of hedging plants named in Appendix I the various possibilities of their use are many.

Yet, when space is available surely there is no finer use of hedges in isolation than the long walk of rigid hornbeams above grass leading through a simple and beautiful gate leading to the sky that we find at Hidcote Manor.

ABOVE: Parterre at Cliveden (page 57)

BELOW: Box spiral, Malcolm House, Batsford (page 55)

ABOVE: The box maze at Gayhurst (page 57)

BELOW: The box parterre at Seaton Delaval (page 58)

Planting Lists

PLANTS FOR LIMY SOILS

The gardener's practical test of the degree of liminess of the soil is when rhododendrons suffer chlorosis, turn yellow and die. Rhododendrons, however, are very choosy, and many plants not growing on lime will thrive where they will not, unless the soil is both shallow and chalky. The following list includes a number that will stand these extreme conditions. Even so, the ground should be well worked and peat or compost incorporated before planting. These plants will grow just as well on neutral or acid soils:

Acer (those kinds named in this book)
Arbutus
Berberis
Buxus
Carpinus
Cephalotaxus
Chamaecyparis
Cotoneaster
Crataegus
Cupressocyparis
Cupressus
Elaeagnus

Erica (certain kinds— see list)
Escallonia
Euonymus
Fagus
Griselinia
Hedera
Ilex
Juniperus
Lavandula
Ligustrum
Lonicera
Osmanthus

Osmarea
Phillyrea
Podocarpus
Prunus
Pyracantha
Querercus ilex
Rosa
Rosmarinus
Ruta
Santolina
Syringa
Taxus
Tilia
Viburnum

PLANTS FOR THE SEASIDE

Seaside conditions involve strong, salt-laden gales which eventually destroy many kinds of plants. On the other hand, particularly on the south and west coasts, extremely low temperatures are rare, and it is possible to grow by the seaside many plants on the borderline of hardiness. Good seaside plants include:

Arbutus	Euonymus	Ligustrum
Cupressocyparis	Fuchsia	Olearia
Cupressus	Griselina	Quercus
Elaeagnus	Hedera	Rhamnus
Erica	Hippophae	Rosmarinus
Escallonia	Lavandula	Tamarix
		Ulex

GENERAL LIST

ACER (*Aceraceae*)

The maples are little if at all used in ornamental hedges, though the hedgerow maple (*A. campestre*) is still found, particularly in limestone districts, as its name implies. It stands pruning and does not "bleed" sap as is usual in the genus. The leaves colour well, usually turning clear yellow, before they fall.

ARBUTUS (*Ericaceae*)

The strawberry tree (*A. unedo*) is an evergreen shrub or small spreading tree which, though recommended as a hedge by Moses Cook as long ago as 1676 on account of its flowers and scarlet fruit occurring simultaneously in autumn, as well as handsome foliage, seems now to be very rarely used for that purpose. It might well provide a decorative, roughly pruned screen (it stands cutting) in all but the coldest districts, particularly near the sea. It is also one of the few ericaceous plants to thrive on a soil containing lime. Propagation is easy from seed, the "strawberries" being dried and then crumbled up. The seedlings are somewhat tender for a couple of years. They can be planted out when about 30 to 60 cm high at 1 m or rather more apart.

ARTEMISIA (*Compositae*)

The southernwood, *A. abrotanum,* with erect stems about 1 m high, densely covered with finely divided, fragrant leaves, is a deciduous plant on the border line of shrubbiness that was formerly much more cultivated than today, particularly in cottage gardens both in country and town (withstanding polluted atmospheres). The insignificant flowers are seldom produced. It needs a sunny position and thrives in poor soil. It makes a good low hedge comparable with rosemary. It is easily propagated from cuttings taken in the summer.

AUCUBA (*Cornaceae*)

The typically Victorian *A. japonica* 'Variegata' was, owing to its ability to grow in the densest shade, poorest ground and most heavily polluted atmospheres, often grown as a hedge, for which its large leaves make it unsuitable unless carefully pruned instead of slashed by shears. The male and female flowers are on separate plants, the handsome berries needing the near-by presence of a male plant. The unvariegated type is, indeed, a handsome large evergreen shrub, but not ideally suited for hedges. Aucubas are propagated from cuttings with the greatest ease.

AZARA (*Flacourtiaceae*)

This delightfully tidy, neat-leaved evergreen shrub, with small flowers, strongly scented with vanilla opening in earliest spring, might surely be used for a hedge in the mildest parts of the country, though I have no knowledge that it ever has been. It is propagated easily from cuttings.

BERBERIS (*Berberidaceae*)

The barberries have for long, and particularly at the present time, been recommended for hedging of various heights. Some are evergreen, some deciduous, some have beauty on account of their myriads of small flowers while others owe their attraction to sprays of orange or red, usually translucent, berries. All have insidious, usually three-pronged spines which makes the necessary weeding, particularly among the deciduous kinds, more than unpleasant. The use of weed killers during the dormant season is largely ineffective, as the bushy growth of the shrubs prevents their proper application; with the evergreen kinds it is, of course, impossible. In no kind known to me is the foliage sufficiently dense to inhibit weed growth. Berberis hedges should therefore be attempted only in weed-free, regularly cultivated ground. Even so, most have a tuft-like bushy growth which leaves the base of a hedge bare.

Bearing these facts in mind, there is not one of the kinds usually listed by nurserymen that might not be tried, from the large-growing and spreading *B. stenophylla* through the cultivars of *B. thunbergii* down to the neat and not unsatisfactory *B. buxifolia nana*. Propagation of the hybrids and cultivars is by division and of the fruiting species by the abundantly borne berries, though seedlings do not always come "true".

BUXUS (*Buxaceae*)

B. sempervirens, the common box, has in its many variants for many centuries been a staple for evergreen hedges and small-scale topiary. It is a hardy shrub of wide distribution, naturally found on chalk, but thriving on any soil that is not water-logged, either in full sun or in considerable shade. It is unharmed by the most severe cutting. As noted by Parkinson, it has, when used for example as an edging to a border, a great disadvantage in the dense mat of roots that spreads outwards from it. From a hedge that had been established some years of about 60 cm high the roots were found to spread some 1·2 m into the surrounding border.*

In its natural form the species makes a small tree, occasionally reaching 9 m. This, presumably, was usually chosen for topiary work. The beautiful weeping form 'Pendula' is also tree-like.

The form used for edging is of very early origin and is known as 'Suffruticosa'. Some strains today are not satisfactory; they have a virus infection. It may be severely clipped to a few inches high, but uncut it will exceed a metre. Pruning should be done in late spring.

There are many variants with variegated and other abnormal leaves, but few seem to be available today.

Box has a most distinctive odour quite unlike that of other plants: it is prevalent in hot weather.

Propagation is by division or cuttings of short young shoots taken under glass in summer.

CARPINUS (*Corylaceae*)

Hornbeam, *C. betulus*, has a long history for use in ornamental work; Moses Cook has already been quoted. James described it and its uses accurately: "Hornbeam has much conformity with the beech, their bark and leaf being very much alike. It is fit, as the beech is, to form walks, palisades and woods; but especially palisades, in which it is made use of more than any other plant. Then the French change its name, and instead of *Charme*, call it *Charmille*, which imports no more than small plants of horn-beam about two foot high, and no bigger than a wheat straw. It bears no fruit but abundance of seed, which is very tedious to raise; its wood is very good to burn."

* Philip Miller regarded this as an advantage; it prevented the soil from being washed out of the borders.

Restoration at
Pitmedden (page 58)

Pleached 'tunnel' being
formed at St. Fagan's
Castle (page 59)

Irish yews at Daneway House (page 58)

Irish yews at Dartington Hall (page 58)

The tediousness of raising refers to the fact that the seed does not germinate until the second spring after sowing. It is then slow growing. Loudon states that it was raised both by the French and Germans from layers.

It is native on sandy or loamy clays in England but will grow on all well-drained soils. The French used to plant it very close, apparently digging it up and re-planting every few years when using it for their dwarf hedges. In Britain on suitable soils, it makes a more attractive and more finely twigged hedge than beech and does not suffer from the aphis that attacks that species. The bark is at first smooth, like that of the beech, but becomes scaly with age. It may be planted about 40–60 cm apart. Pruning should be done in midsummer; if done in spring it bleeds. The cultivar 'Fastigiata', not very accurately named, is a beautifully formed pyramidal tree well suited to formal designs.

CARYOPTERIS (*Verbenaceae*)

C. clandonensis is a vigorous small shrub with grey aromatic leaves bearing bright blue flowers in late summer and early autumn. It stands clipping well and might make a delightful low hedge of, say, 75 cm. It prefers light soil and needs a sunny, open situation.

CORYLUS (*Corylaceae*)

As the hazel *C. avellana* is, with its delightful catkins heralding spring, a feature of our wild hedgerows, surely this might be used in ornamental hedges, perhaps in the cultivar 'Aurea' with pale yellow leaves. The stronger-growing filbert, *C. maxima*, has a very handsome richly purple-leaved form 'Purpurea'—the catkins are also purple—which it has been suggested can be effectively contrasted with the foregoing. Those forms of hazel which do not come true from seed (this does not germinate until the second spring after sowing) can be propagated from the division of suckers or layering. These hazels will thrive on all types of soil.

COTONEASTER (*Rosaceae*)

There are a number of this genus, both evergreen and deciduous, which are suitable for hedges. The flowers, which are very numerous and attract bees in large numbers, are not particularly interesting, but the usually red berries which follow are most decorative—though enjoyed by birds. The best for a clipped, formal hedge is *C. simonsii*, a semi-evergreen of close, erect growth. *C. franchettii* and its variety *sternianus* (sometimes miscalled *wardii*) are evergreen shrubs reaching some 3 m, making good informal hedges with orange-red berries; the leaves are grey underneath. *C. salicifolius* is another evergreen with tall, arching stems and bright red berries: 'Fructu-luteo' has yellow berries. All these are hardy and will grow well on any soil, including chalk, providing it is not waterlogged. They can be propagated from cuttings from half-ripened shoots taken in July or from seed: some kinds produce many self-sown seedlings. Young plants should be set about 60 cm apart.

CRATAEGUS (*Rosaceae*)

The common hawthorn of our hedgerows, *C. monogyna*, is the thorniest of all. It is easy to establish when planted out when young, seedlings having previously been once transplanted. They should be set fairly close—not more than 30 cm apart. Pruning and clipping is usually done in autumn or winter. There are several other species and cultivars more decorative than this thorn as trees, but it is doubtful if they have any advantage over our native kind for hedging. The oriental thorn, *C. orientalis*, without many spines and silvery leaves, particularly when young, is a possible variation: the large orange-red berries are good.

CYTISUS (*Leguminosae*)

There are several erect growing species such as *C. albus*, *C. scoparius* and *C. nigricans*, as well as many named hybrids which are suitable for rough hedges in open situations and which thrive on light sandy soil. Most should be trimmed immediately after flowering, taking care not to cut into the old wood. An exception is *C. nigricans*, which should be pruned quite hard in early spring to encourage the new growth on which flowers arise later in the summer. Brooms can be raised from seed—it is worth sowing it from the hybrids, though these may not come true —or from cuttings taken in August. Plants must be put out when small, as the root system is sparse.

DAPHNE (*Thymelaeaceae*)

As has been mentioned, Moses Cook recommended the use of *D. mezereum*, both the purple-red and white flowered forms, mixed, as a hedge: the sweet scent of the flowers on the leafless shoots in earliest spring or even late winter is delightful. Having an erect growth in suitable conditions sometimes considerably exceeding 1 m, it might well be so used today, bearing in mind that it will not tolerate pruning. It is happier when the base of the bush is shaded by some low-growing plant. Seedlings are easily raised and must be planted out when small, as the plant strongly resents root disturbance. Perhaps 30 cm would be the correct distance. The white form with yellow berries usually comes true from seed. An attractive low hedge in severe shade could be made of the handsome evergreen *D. laureola*, the spurge laurel, not infrequently found growing in the heart of woods on limestone and chalk. The glossy leaves are up to 10 cm long. The insignificant yellow flowers have a fugitive scent. This also reaches about 1 m and is much longer lived than *D. mezereon*.

DEUTZIA (*Hydrangeaceae*)

The vigorous, hardy and very erect-growing deciduous *D. scabra*, soon reaching 3 m or more on any kind of soil, would make an excellent hedge of that height when planted say 1 m or rather less apart. It should not be topped; pruning should consist of thinning out wood immediately after it has flowered in June. There are several forms. 'Candidissima', the tallest grower, has double white flowers; 'Plena' or 'Pride of Rochester' has double flowers suffused on the outside with rose.

ELAEAGNUS (*Elaeagnaceae*)

While unsuitable for formal clipping, several kinds are excellent as broad, spreading and decorative protective hedges withstanding wind and seaside conditions. The evergreen *E. ebbingei* is tall, strong growing and particularly wind-firm and evergreen, the leaves being silvery on the under side. Also good is *E. macrophylla*, another evergreen whose leaves are at first silvery and with small flowers in autumn which are pleasantly scented. *E. pungens* is itself not distinguished; taller than the others, it has in its cultivars the rather smaller 'Maculata' ('Aureo-variegata') and to a lesser extent 'Argentea-variegata' two of the most handsome hardy variegated shrubs in cultivation. All will grow in a variety of soils. Propagation is by cuttings or layering; pot-grown plants are easiest to establish. Being spreading, they may be planted up to 1 m apart.

ERICA (*Ericaceae*)

The tree heaths make good informal hedges in or around heath gardens or by the sea. *E. arborea,* the tree heath, is the tallest of all being in suitable conditions tree-like, but only satisfactory in the milder parts of Britain. The honey-scented flowers are white and lavishly produced in early spring. It thrives best on light acid soil and will not tolerate lime. A hardier, more erect but smaller form is *E. arborea alpina*. Needing similar conditions but of more erect growth and also with white flowers is *E. canaliculata*. *E. lusitanica* is also not dissimilar in the conditions it needs, flowering earlier than *E. arborea*.

Both hardy and lime tolerant, though reaching only some 1·2 m is *E. mediterranea*, a valuable plant with rosy red flowers from early to late spring; the white form 'W. T. Rackliff' is of more compact growth also hardy and adaptable is *E. terminalis*, 1 m or a little more high, with pink flowers at the ends of the shoots in late summer. The numerous other species and garden forms of *Erica* are both too small and by nature too spreading for use in hedges. Propagation is easy from short shoots taken as cuttings in sandy soil in late summer which root freely. The species can be raised from seed. No more than light trimming is required. All should be planted close together. (See also p. 50).

ESCALLONIA (*Escalloniaceae*)

The escallonias are spreading evergreen shrubs with arching branches bearing small leaves and a multitude of small flowers in late summer and early autumn, much visited by bees, ranging from white to carmine. All are tolerant of a wide range of soils and are particularly successful under seaside conditions, particularly those that are not entirely hardy in cold districts. Most of those in cultivation are hybrids, of which there are many. They range in height from about 1·5 m to 2·5 m. The following are recommended:

'C. F. Ball' grows tall and has crimson flowers.

'Donard Brilliance' with large rose-red flowers.

Edinensis is a smaller bush with rose-pink flowers and is very hardy.

Exoniensis is an old hybrid, tall growing, with white to pale pink flowers opening over a long period.

Ingramii is a tall-growing shrub with deep pink flowers and is recommended for hedging by the sea.

Iveyi has good, glossy foliage and white flowers in autumn.

Langleyensis is one of the hardiest about 2 m high with rose-crimson flowers.

Macrantha is a strong grower, 2 m or more high and one of the best wind-breaks for the milder counties by the sea, but not always hardy inland; the leaves are glossy and the flowers rosy-red.

Punctata is a tall grower of vigorous habit with deep crimson flowers withstanding sea winds in the mild counties.

All are easily propagated from cuttings. They should be planted about 60 cm apart. They are not suitable for close clipping, but if necessary can be rough pruned by removing branches after they have flowered.

EUONYMUS (*Celastraceae*)

The common spindle, occasionally reaching the size of a small tree with its red fruit splitting to expose the seeds in their orange-coloured covering, together with the brilliant purplish and red autumn foliage, is a decorative feature of many hedgerows on limestone formations. It will be noticed, however, that plants are not bushy at the base and also that it is prone to be badly attacked by black-fly—the cure being winter spraying with tar-oil wash. It might well be used mixed with other hedging plants, particularly on acid soils, where it does not arise naturally. A white-fruited form, 'Alba', and one called 'Atropurpurea', with purplish leaves turning bright red in autumn, are available. The type is propagated by seed and variants from cuttings which root easily.

E. japonica with its glossy evergreen leaves is one of the commonest hedges in seaside gardens, particularly in the south and west; it is not hardy in colder districts. It will reach 3·5 m and more. It stands clipping well, and should be planted about ·5 m apart. It is easily rooted from cuttings.

FAGUS (*Fagaceae*)

The common beech, *F. sylvatica*, the best tree for use on calcareous, particularly chalk, soils is admirable and widely used for hedges. In the juvenile state it retains its leaves, which turn russet in the autumn, until they are forced off by the new growth in mid-May. This phenomenon is retained (as with hornbeam) when the tree is regularly clipped, however old it may be. Provided this is regularly done, a beech hedge can be grown to and maintained at a considerable height. Curiously, its use as a clipped hedge is not mentioned by early authors such as Evelyn and d'Argenville or even by Loudon; hornbeam seems always to have been preferred for clipping. Close-planted beech was recommended for tall palisades. It was also recommended for avenues.

The shoots produce closely twigged, flat sprays of foliage which intermesh, making a close, dense growth. This rigid form, however, makes it unsuitable for topiary.

How narrow an old hedge can be is shown, facing page 81. This also suggests that with a trunk that will grow to this diameter, it is not necessary to plant it as close as is the usual practice, which is about 45 cm to 60 cm apart. To make a very substantial hedge two rows may be used, the plants staggered, at about 60 cm apart. Plants between 40 and 60 cm may be used. Beech is always raised from seed, which germinates freely. In districts where self-sown seedlings abound it is possible to lift seedlings at the end of their first year's growth by means of a bulb planter. The wads so lifted with the seedling in the centre are then lined out in well-dug ground and in two years (or they can be left for three) are ready to plant out. Seedlings of copper or purple beeches can be raised giving a considerable range of colours and used to make an attractive vari-coloured hedge.

Clipping should be done in summer, when the new foliage has grown.

FUCHSIA (*Onagraceae*)

Fuchsias of several kinds can be used for hedges in mild and particularly seaside districts. They flower freely in late summer and autumn, even the more tender kinds which are often apparently killed in winter but shoot up again when cut down to ground-level. The hardiest and that which is most often seen growing vigorously in seaside hedges is *F. magellanica*, with slender stems and narrow red and purple flowers. The form known as 'Riccartoni' is the most vigorous; "Alba" with off-white flowers is not so large nor is the attractive 'Versicolor' with leaves marked in pink, crimson and cream. As fuchsias flower on current year's wood, they should be pruned early in the year. Cuttings strike easily under glass.

GRISELINIA (*Cornaceae*)

G. littoralis is a large evergreen shrub with leathery, shining yellowish-green leaves which only thrives in mild districts, and particularly by the sea, where it with-stands strong winds and salt spray, is used for hedging. The insignificant male and female flowers are on separate plants. Propagation is easy from cuttings taken in late summer in gentle heat. They may be planted out at, say, 1 m apart. Reaching some 2·5 m, it needs little or no pruning. It grows well on chalk.

HEBE (*Scrophulariaceae*)

The "shrubby veronicas" are evergreens which for the most part are not reliably hardy except in mild districts near the sea. There are some fifty kinds, many of them hybrids, several of which no doubt might be well suited to provide interesting low hedges in maritime conditions—though some have brittle stems and cannot withstand strong wind. All are easily propagated and produce their decorative spikes of flowers ranging from white to various shades in and around blue. The hybrid called usually *H. elliptica* but more correctly *H. francisciana* 'Latifolia', with mauve flowers and reaching about 1 m, is not infrequently seen as a low, in-formal seaside hedge needing little pruning other than the cutting out of dead wood.

HEDERA (*Araliaceae*)

The ivy is not usually considered as a hedging plant, but there is no reason why the so called "tree ivy" should not provide a valuable evergreen hedge which will stand some trimming and reach a height of, say, 1 m. Tree ivy is, in fact, no more than the flowering growth of the common ivy, *H. helix*, which when it has reached the top of its support, whether it be a wall or a tree, produces unlobed leaves and flowers. Cuttings of this state root very easily if taken in late summer and almost always (but not invariably as stated in most books) retain the adult bushy form and flower freely in October. When the variegated and other coloured forms of ivy produce this adult growth, they may likewise be propagated. The young plants may be set out at about 40 cm apart. Pruning should be done in late summer.

HIBISCUS (*Malvaceae*)

The tree hollyhocks are erect-growing deciduous shrubs, being mostly cultivated forms of *H. syriacus*, which has hollyhock-like flowers in late summer and autumn. They are usually grown in sunny, sheltered places, such as against a wall, to ensure ripening of the wood and protection of the late flowers. I have never seen them used for hedging, but include them here on account of Loudon's statement in 1838: "It forms beautiful garden hedges, more especially when the different sorts are planted in a harmonious order of succession, according to their colours; and when the plants are not clipped, but carefully pruned with the knife." (At that time seedlings of the single sorts were selling in London at 50s. a hundred!)

HIPPOPHAE (*Elaeagnaceae*)

H. rhamnoides, the sea buckthorn, is a tall deciduous shrub occasionally reaching the size of a small, straggling tree noted for its hardiness and ability to thrive in almost any kind of soil and under most conditions, including gales by the seashore. The willow-like leaves have a distinct silvery sheen. The orange berries are decorative, long-lasting and produced in large quantities in early autumn on the female plants only, making them extremely attractive for some months. It is said that one male should be planted, preferably to the windward, of six females. The males can be identified by the pollen that can be shaken from the very small flowers in April. This shrub is ideal as an extremely decorative free-growing hedge for the seaside or for that matter in any other situation.

ILEX (*Aquifoliaceae*)

Evelyn's description of the use of our common holly, *I. aquifolium*, describes in glowing terms the merit of this, one of our very few native evergreen trees (for such it is, occasionally reaching 20 m or even more) as a hedge plant. There were variegated forms in his day; a century after his death it was claimed that there were about forty variants, most with differing leaf markings. Today there are some thirty different kinds available. Almost invariably, and indeed the most suitable kind for ordinary hedging, the normal type is used—having as a distinct disadvantage that if near a flower-bed there seems no defence against the sharp spines of the fallen leaves when weeding. If berries are required, the male and female flowers are on separate plants and it is necessary to raise plants from a known female. Generally, there is a male tree in the neighbourhood to provide pollen, but this must be checked. The flowers open in mid May: the male has four prominent pollen-covered stamens and no style, the female a prominent style and small, rudimentary anthers without pollen. Pollination is very effectively carried out by bees who work very actively in the flowers of both sexes in search of nectar. Of the variegated kinds, the following are usually listed: 'Argenteo-marginata' silver, female; 'Golden King' broad-leaved, not very spiny and with a yellow margin to the leaves, female; 'Silver Queen', large leaves with creamy-white variegation, male. A dwarf, slow-growing form which is very spiny and which would make an attractive low hedge is 'Recurva'.

In addition to these forms of the native holly, there is a series of what are called the broad-leaved hollies which are particularly handsome. They originated as hybrids between the not entirely hardy Canary Islands holly, *I. perado*, introduced in 1760, and our native species. The first, giving its name to the series, was the male *I. altaclarensis*—the Highclere holly—which was in cultivation by 1838 and has large leaves with variable spines and is of vigorous growth. From it have arisen the extremely handsome female and almost spineless 'Camelliaefolia' and the male 'Hodginsii', often said to be the best of all hollies for hedging, with its glossy leaves and purple stems. No satisfactory variegated forms of the *I. alta-clarensis* series exist.

Propagation of the species *I. aquifolium* is from seed which does not germinate until the second spring after sowing, while all the others are raised from cuttings of half-ripe wood taken in July or August. Planting out is best done at the usual time for evergreens with plants between ·5 and 1 m high. The ground should be well prepared, the plants set at about 40 cm to 75 cm apart and well watered in. Quite often newly planted hollies lose their leaves, which usually shows that they have taken root.

Hollies are tolerant of a wide range of soils, often growing in nature on light, gravelly, acid ground, but all benefit from good cultivation. They will not stand stagnant moisture. They will also thrive (as is often seen in woodlands) in moderate shade. Pruning is best done in April or any convenient time except in winter, when exceptional cold may cause browning and even leaf fall. One advantage of April

LEFT: Pleached limes at Wickham Market, Suffolk (page 60)

BELOW LEFT: Lime palisade at Wallington (page 60)

BELOW RIGHT: Ash 'tunnel' at Regents Park (page 60)

The long hedges, Hidcote Manor (page 64)

'Stilt' hedges, Hidcote Manor (page 60)

pruning is that subsequent growth hides blemishes such as leaves damaged by the shears. The individual leaves usually last four years, mostly falling in July or occasionally as the consequence of severe weather.

From time to time hollies are badly affected by the holly leaf miner whose small grubs live within the leaves, giving them a blotched appearance. In my experience this infestation occurs only periodically, and often at long intervals, sufficiently badly to make the bushes unsightly: it is due to a small fly. In some years, too, the grub of a moth binds the leaves on the young shoots together and eats them. This also only occurs to any extent intermittently.

LAURUS (*Lauraceae*)

L. nobilis, the bay, is in this country usually a handsome evergreen shrub or small tree with aromatic foliage that is only really hardy in our mild districts, when it is usually seen as a specimen cut into a simple shape. More often, it is grown in tubs which are put indoors during the winter. It stands clipping well. A narrow-leaved form, 'Angustifolia', is said to be hardier than the type. It can be raised from imported seeds or from the berries produced in the milder districts or from layers.

LAVANDULA (*Labiatae*)

Lavender, *L. spica*, is an evergreen shrub of naturally erect growth, the narrow leaves of which are covered with down which at first is almost white but becomes grey. The flower spikes come in late summer and for centuries have been famous for their long-lasting scent, found to a lesser extent in the leaves. It stands clipping well and indeed free-growing bushes should be sheared over to remove the dead flowers. It has long been used for clipped edgings. There are several variants in commerce. 'Grappenhall Variety' is the tallest, reaching 1 m. The popular 'Munstead Dwarf' is said to have been improved on by 'Folgate'. 'Nana Atropurpurea', better known as 'Hidcote', has deep violet flowers. All lavenders need a sunny place, the warmer the better, and do well by the seaside. Any severe pruning for shaping the bushes is best done in April. Propagation is from cuttings which root easily in late summer.

LIGUSTRUM (*Oleaceae*)

The privet is one of the most abused of all hedging plants, because of its use in unsuitable and unlikeable situations and on account of the heavy, unpleasant odour of its flowers in late summer and its voracious, spreading root system. These criticisms when applied to the genus as a whole are only partially correct.

L. delavayanum (*ionandrum*) is a very hardy, neat-leaved evergreen shrub, growing to about 2 m high, rather spreading, but easily cut into shape as a low hedge. The very numerous small clusters of white flowers in June, with prominent violet anthers, have no heavy scent. They are followed by masses of small black berries from which it is easily raised—in fact it seeds itself.

L. japonicum is a very spreading, large-leaved evergreen privet which might be suggested for hedges, but its chief merit lies in a massive production, covering the bush, of large, broad flower spikes of flowers with the heavy privet scent in late July and August. Its foliage may be badly damaged in severe winters.

L. lucidum has the finest foliage of all privets, the leaves being rich green and about 10 cm long. It flowers in September. Reaching 5 or 6 m and sometimes 10 m in height and tree-like in form, it might well be used to form a splendid, tall hedge. There are striking variegated forms which are not often seen. This species unfortunately rarely produces fruit in this country.

L. ovalfolium is the commonest, semi-evergreen privet in cultivation. Almost without attractions, it will grow in the worst possible situations, including the poorest soils, from which it will extract the last traces of nutriment. Its form 'Aureomarginatum' ('Aureum'), the golden privet is an outstandingly effective golden-leaved shrub. The much less common 'Argenteum' with creamy white variegation has an attractive ghost-like quality.

L. vulgare, the native privet, is not worth while growing: it drops its leaves in winter.

Privets are easily raised from seed when it is produced or from cuttings taken in late summer. All those named above will grow in any soil that is reasonably fertile and not waterlogged. Plants should be set about ·5 m apart, except *L. lucidum* which might go in at about 1 m. *L. ovalifolium* should be cut back hard after planting.

LONICERA (*Caprifoliaceae*)

Hardly recognizable as a honeysuckle, *L. nitida* is an evergreen, twiggy bush with leaves no more than 1·5 cm long. It grows quickly and stands clipping well and will soon make a dense hedge of about 1·5 m high. It can, however, be badly damaged in winter in cold localities and with age becomes bare at the base. It will thrive on all well-drained soils. It is easily propagated from cuttings taken in late summer. Plants should be set out at about 30 cm apart. They should be clipped during summer; then probably twice or even oftener later in the year. It can be used for small-sized topiary work.

OLEARIA (*Compositae*)

There are a number of these evergreen Australasian daisy bushes that might be used as hedging plants, particularly in seaside situations where they thrive under the mild conditions. *O. haastii* is hardy with dense, dull green foliage consisting of leathery leaves about 2 cm long and bearing numerous small daisy-like flowers in late summer which leave untidy brownish seed heads. It reaches about 2 m in height, stands pruning well and is happy under urban conditions.

O. macrodonta is a much more handsome shrub, perfectly hardy in most winters in the Midlands; when damaged by exceptionally severe frost it breaks again from the base. The large, leathery leaves are wavy and holly-like. It flowers heavily in June with white daisy flowers much larger than in *O. haastii*; they are scented. The bushes will reach the size of a small tree in exceptionally mild climates, but will stand pruning well. The form in cultivation is 'Major'.

Olearias are propagated by cuttings taken in late summer. They need acid soils. As those named make spreading bushes fairly quickly, they might be planted about 1 m apart.

OSMANTHUS (*Oleaceae*)

This genus of evergreen shrubs with small, white, sweetly scented flowers includes several that are suitable for hedges of moderate height. Those named below are hardy, stand pruning well, grow in any well-drained soil and can be propagated from cuttings taken in late summer.

O. delavayi is a compact, rather slow-growing shrub eventually reaching about 2 m. It has neat, dark green leaves. In mid-April it is thickly covered with sweetly scented white flowers like minute trumpets. It stands clipping well. It tends to be broader than the height and could be planted about 40 cm apart. It should be clipped after flowering.

O. heterophyllus is a hybrid whose origin is shown by the leaves ranging from those like a small holly to those with entire margins—the parents being *O. aquifolium* and *O. illicfolius*. The mature foliage is a rich green, the young shoots and leaves being bronze coloured. The small, white, scented flowers open in September and October. It is slow growing and should be planted about 45 cm apart. Clipping should be done in late summer.

OSMAREA (*Oleaceae*)

O. burkwoodii is a hybrid raised between *Osmanthus delavayi* and *Phillyrea decora* (see below) which forms a slow-growing evergreen bush with narrow leathery leaves about 4 cm long that are slightly toothed and dark green. The flowers are white, borne in small clusters in April and sweetly scented. It is very hardy, stands clipping well and is easily propagated from cuttings. It should make a good, dense hedge.

PALIURUS (*Rhamnaceae*)

P. spina-christi, Christ's thorn, was, Loudon tells us (perhaps it still is) widely used for hedges in Italy and the south of France. It is a deciduous shrub with distinct three-nerved leaves about 4 cm. long, small yellow flowers insignificant individually but quite striking owing to their large numbers during late summer. The fruit is extraordinary in resembling a broad-brimmed hat. The shrubs bear two kinds of thorn, one less than 1 cm long and the other much smaller. The thin flexible branches become closely intertwined. It is quite hardy, needs little trimming and is easily raised from imported seeds. It is not particular as to soil.

PHILLYREA (*Oleaceae*)

Two species of this genus, *P. angustifolia* and *P. media*, hardy evergreen shrubs with opposite flowers were early introductions and frequently planted in the days when few evergreens were available. They were, said Evelyn, often grown in greenhouses and stoves whereas, he pointed out, they are quite as hardy as holly; he mentions variegated kinds. Loudon wrote: "It was formerly . . . in much repute for covering naked walls, and clipping into figures of balls, men, animals, etc. The largest phillyrea hedge in England is said to be at Brampton Park, near Huntingdon, the seat of lady Olivia B. Sparrow." Making small and tidy trees if left uncut, both species and their varieties are very neglected today. *P. angustifolia* with narrow leaves about 5 cm long and with dull white scented flowers in May and June has a variety *rosmarinifolia* with smaller, narrower leaves somewhat glaucous in colour. *P. latifolia* is larger in all its parts, the dark, glossy leaves being 3 cm or so broad, and toothed; it has two varieties, *ilicifolia* with much more sharply toothed leaves and *rotundifolia* with rounder leaves.

These are the phillyreas of the old writers, but by far the best is *P. decora* introduced in 1867. It has dense foliage of a rich green, with broadly lance-shaped leaves about 12 cm long. The flowers are pure white in dense clusters opening in April. It is extremely hardy and a most valuable evergreen shrub.

PRUNUS (*Rosaceae*)

This large genus into which botanists surprisingly bundle almonds, apricots, cherries, peaches and cherry laurels includes a number of good hedging and screening plants.

P. blieriana is a large deciduous, bushy shrub, well furnished at the base, with purple leaves and small double pink flowers in late March. This makes a good

ABOVE: *Ulmus campestris Camperdownii* (page 60)

BELOW: *Cotoneaster franchettii* (page 69)

ABOVE: A fine old beech hedge,
Edinburgh Botanic Garden (page 73)

LEFT: A cross-section of the
same hedge

BELOW: *Lonicera nitida* used
for topiary (page 78)

informal screen, needing little pruning, up to 3 m and planted, say, 1·5 m. apart.

P. cerasifera, the cherry plum or myrobalan, is a small, very twiggy deciduous tree with small white flowers in March or even February. It is sometimes found in fruit-growing districts planted as a screen, giving in favourable seasons a crop ripening in July of yellow or red fruit. It makes a good, close hedge up to 2 m or more if kept hard clipped. The celebrated cv. with crimson-purple leaves is known as 'Pissardii' or more correctly 'Atropurpurea'. It should be planted about 1 m apart. Clipping should be done when dormant.

P. incisa, the Fuji cherry, a small-growing deciduous tree usually with several stems, is illustrated in Collingwood Ingram's *Ornamental Cherries*, growing and flowering freely, with its white flowers opening from pink buds in March, as a hard clipped hedge some 2 m high planted about 1 m apart. The leaves colour a deep yellow in autumn. It produces black, pea-like fruit in some years, which germinate freely. Unfortunately in some districts bull-finches destroy the flower buds.

P. insititia. The growing of damsons as free standards along roadsides and as avenues in orchard rides is an old practice not, unfortunately, much carried out today. It is a very hardy tree, the white, sweetly scented flowers opening on the otherwise bare twigs making such plantings a delightful sight.

P. laurocerasus. The cherry-laurel with its fine dark, glossy, evergreen leaves has suffered much maltreatment in gardens. Naturally, a spreading small tree, which is handsome when left unpruned, it may be grown as an attractive, dense hedge only if its shoots are individually pruned with secateurs to avoid damaging the leaves. Admittedly a laborious proceeding, this is best done in summer after the growth is completed. Planting should be perhaps 1·5 m apart. It is greedy and robs the neighbouring soil. A slow-growing form with leaves only some 15 cm by 4 cm, 'Zabelliana', stands pruning well and might make an attractive low hedge, flowering in mid-May and again in autumn. Propagation is from late summer cuttings preferably with some heat. The Portugal laurel (*P. lusitanica*) is probably best grown unpruned as a specimen; I have never seen it succeeding as a hedge.

P. spinosa, the native blackthorn or sloe, a suckering, often thicket-forming deciduous shrub, growing well on alkaline soils and flowering freely from March onwards, might well be introduced into rough hedges.

PYRACANTHA (*Rosaceae*)

The evergreen firethorns, of which the European species *P. coccinea* with scarlet berries is mentioned by Parkinson as suitable for hedges. He calls it the "prickly coral tree".

P. atalantioides is the tallest growing and will stand shade. *P. coccinea* 'Lalandii' has orange-red berries.

They can be grown free and roughly pruned or as formal hedges. In this case they must be trained to wires between posts, as otherwise they sprawl and become gappy. The long shoots are best cut after growth has finished; there will be plenty of berries left. Planting should be about 1 m or rather more apart, and as with all evergreens in early autumn or late spring.

QUERCUS (*Fagaceae*)

The evergreen holm oak, *Querius ilex*, has the merit of thriving in seaside conditions and on calcareous ground as long as it is well drained. Particularly when young it will not, however, stand severe cold. A hedge at Mount Edgcumbe near Plymouth when 150 or more years old exceeded 9 m in height.

This oak is readily raised from acorns, which must be sown as soon as, or even a little before, they are ripe. A tap root is soon formed, so that seedlings should be planted out in their second year either in early autumn or late spring. Probably 1 m apart is satisfactory spacing. Pruning should be done when the young growth is complete in summer and after the leaves, which last two or three years, have fallen.

RHAMNUS (*Rhamnaceae*)

The alaternus, *R. alaternus*, is rarely seen in gardens today, yet was once a highly prized evergreen. Parkinson wrote that it "groweth not to be a tree of any height; but abiding lowe, spreadeth forth many branches, whereon are set many divers small and hard greene leaves, somewhat round for the forme, and endented a little by the edges: it beareth many whitish green flowers at the joynts of the stalkes, and setting on of the lower leaves clustering thicke together, which after turne into small blacke berries, wherein are contained many small graines or seeds: the beauty and verdure of these leaves abiding so fresh all the yeare, doth cause it to be of the greater respect; and therefore findeth place in their Gardens onely, that are curious conservers of all nature beauties".

In 1706 London and Wise in their adaptation from the French, *The Retir'd Gardener*, recommend that it should be grown in boxes and "you give it what shape you think fit by the help of your shears, which, being well guided, will make this shrub of a very agreeable figure" for ornamenting gardens and courtyards and placing in the borders of parterres. I have never seen it so used.

By 1740, in his *Gardener's Dictionary*, Philip Miller wrote that it was very common in old gardens and formerly in much request to make evergreen hedges, but it was now almost wholly disused for that purpose, growing too quickly and need-ing frequent cutting in summer to keep it handsome and from being displaced by strong winds.

Loudon recommended it for town gardens, as it was less injured by coal smoke than other evergreens. He adds that it is easily propagated from cuttings taken in autumn in sandy soil in a north border under a hand-light. He says that as it is not very productive of fibrous roots, if large plants are required they should be potted up.

Today, *R. alaternus* is recommended as a quick-growing evergreen for exposed coastal gardens. The variant 'Argenteo-variegata' with creamy-white leaf borders is a striking shrub, but not so hardy as the type.

RHODODENDRON (*Ericaceae*)

Rhododendron ponticum is used as a broad hedge kept roughly trimmed, flowering in May and June. Unlike many rhododendrons, it grows naturally in the open and does not need shade. An acid soil is essential. It should be remembered that in some districts if allowed to seed it can become established as a menacing weed difficult to eradicate. The hardier hybrids can also be so used. Seedlings—often plentiful self-sown supplies can be dug up in autumn—planted about 1 m apart will soon unite. The much smaller small-leaved hybrid *R. praecox* is of more upright growth, eventually reaching 1 m or rather more in height. The early flowers are often damaged by frost, but even so it makes a neat, partially deciduous hedge needing little attention. It is easily propagated by cuttings taken in late summer, which when large enough can be planted at about 50 cm apart. A notable hedge of this is in the Royal Botanic Garden, Edinburgh.

R. racemosum, even smaller but evergreen and densely leaved, might make a very good dwarf hedge. It comes easily from seed and cuttings.

ROSMARINUS (*Labiatae*)

Rosemary, it is recorded, was used in the younger Pliny's Laurentian garden when the box died out. It was a favourite of Sir Thomas More in the Thames-side garden that he made at Chelsea in 1520, "not only because his bees loved it but because 'tis the herb sacred to remembrance and therefore to friendship".

Rosmarinus officinalis, the common kind, with grey stems and glossy green, narrow leaves, will form a picturesque old shrub. It also stands clipping well, is happy on chalk and makes an excellent low hedge by the seaside. It needs sun. The evergreen leaves are seldom scorched even in severe winters. The violet-blue flowers are at their best in May. It is easily propagated from September cuttings, which is also probably the best month to trim it. Young plants should be planted about ·5 m apart. It does not need enriched soil. There is a particularly upright form called 'Pyramidalis' or 'Miss Jessup's Upright'. Corsican forms with larger, bluer forms than the type but not so hardy go under several names.

ROSA (*Rosaceae*)

The use of roses in hedging is a large subject and should be treated by skilled rosarians. I am certain that they should be used only when both sides of the hedge are of cultivated ground—having spent many hours over many years of trying to eradicate the larger and most vigorous forms of grass from an ancient hedge of a form of the most beautiful (and freely suckering) Scots rose, optimistically planted to divide an orchard from an area of short-mown grass. Again, apart from thorniness, the rose has no intrinsic merit for hedging; it must be carefully pruned, not clipped, and has but a brief spell in flower. And, as was pointed out by Miss Jekyll as long ago as 1902, a rose hedge will be bare at its base.

I would that I could refer the reader to some rosarian manual dealing adequately with this subject, but alas I cannot.

RUTA (*Rutaceae*)

R. graveolens, rue, is usually grown in the herb garden. It is therefore worth quoting what Loudon wrote: ". . . yet when planted in dry, deep, calcareous soil, and suffered to grow without being cut over, it forms a singularly handsome evergreen shrub, attaining the height of 6 feet or even 8 feet in as many years. The manner in which the leaves are cut, their glaucous hue, the profusion of fine, dark yellow flowers, which are produced for several months in succession, and often throughout the whole winter, justify us in strongly recommending the rue for cultivation as an ornamental plant. It will not succeed, however, if mixed with other trees and shrubs of rampant growth, nor attain a large size, unless in a sheltered situation, and in a soil that is deep, free and calcareous. It forms beautiful evergreen separation hedges for cottage gardens; and some fine hedges of this sort, and also large, single plants may be seen in the bottoms of old chalk pits on the south bank of the Thames, about Gravesend, in Kent. The plant is propagated in the easiest manner, by seeds or cuttings, and requires no other pruning during its whole existence than cutting off the withered flower-stalks. It appears to be a shrub of very great durability."

The form known as 'Jackman's Blue' is bluer than the type and of bushier growth: Messrs Jackman recommend shearing back last season's growth each April and to prevent it from blooming by removing flower spikes if possible.

SANTOLINA (*Compositae*)

Santolina chamaecyparissus, cotton lavender, was well described and recommended by Parkinson (see p. 24) as a dwarf grey-leaved edging for knots. It reaches about ·5 m high, carrying yellow flowers in July (which should be sheared off by the tidy-minded when over). It is not long-lived and becomes ragged. It is easily raised from August cuttings. They should be planted out say ·3 m apart in un-enriched soil. *S. neapolitana* is somewhat larger with more firmly cut leaves, and I think, more attractive than the foregoing.

SARCOCCA (*Buxaceae*)

I have never seen these small, evergreen berrying shrubs used for dwarf hedges, but given a shady or moist site I can imagine nothing more satisfactory. Sending up several shoots from the base until they become quite dense, they bear narrow, glossy leaves. Mostly in late winter they produce insignificant but sweetly scented flowers. They need little clipping. *S. hookeriana digyna* reaches about 1 m and has purple stems; *S. humilis* is half that height and *S. ruscifolia* about 1·2 m. All are hardy and happy in any reasonable soil. Propagation is by division or from August cuttings in frames.

SPIRAEA (*Rosaceae*)

Though I have never seen it done, the dwarf-growing *S. bullata* and *S. bumalda* 'Anthony Waterer' might well be used to make a very dwarf hedge. Loudon has this to say of *S. hypericifolia*, a slender—twigged deciduous shrub of about 6 feet with white flowers in May: "It forms handsome garden hedges, and will bear the shears, which were formerly applied to it, to shape into artificial forms, when topiary work was fashionable . . . It is readily propagated by layers, or detaching its suckers." I have never seen it so used.

SYMPHORICARPUS (*Caprifoliaceae*)

The common white-fruited snowberry, *S. albus* (*racemosus*), is often found growing in hedges, usually of old gardens. It has the merit of thriving under even apparently impossible conditions, the white berries, glistening when first formed, being particularly attractive and persisting for many weeks. *S.a. laevigatus* has larger berries, which weigh down the slender branchlets. *S. orbiculatus* has clusters of pink berries, and has an attractive golden-leaved form 'Variegatus'. Other improved named forms are in cultivation. 'White Hedge' is described as of strong, upright and compact growth, bearing erect trusses of small white berries and a good hedging plant, but as yet seems uncommon in cultivation. All benefit from good cultivation in well-prepared soil, and should be planted about ·5 m apart; propagation is easy from cuttings or by division. The small flowers are visited by large numbers of bees collecting nectar.

SYRINGA (*Oleaceae*)

It is possible but not very satisfactory to make a tall screen of those lilacs which are named cultivars of *S. vulgaris*. The plants must be raised from cuttings on their own roots, otherwise the forest of suckers that will arise will not be true to type. As neither form of growth nor foliage are attractive, only during the short flowering period has such a screen any charm. The lilac, too, is a greedy feeder and does not encourage growth of plants put close to fill the usually bare base.

TAMARIX (*Tamaricaceae*)

Except in seaside districts, tamarisks are much neglected as providers of graceful, free-growing hedging plants thriving in all soils except shallow chalk and preferring a sunny, open position. The small pink flowers are on short shoots arising from the branches covered with small scale-like leaves.

    T. gallica sometimes reaches 3 m. The flowers are pink, opening in late summer and autumn. *T. pentandra*, of about the same height, had glaucous, deciduous foliage and masses of pink flowers giving a display from late summer to autumn. Both the above flower on current season's shoots, so winter pruning consists of cutting flowered wood out. *T. tetrandra* is different in that it produces its pink flowers on the previous year's growth in May, and must be pruned accordingly. Propagation is from stout shoots taken as cuttings in the open ground in early winter, or by even larger shoots driven in where the hedge is to be.

TILIA (*Tiliaceae*)

Of the lime tree or linden Evelyn wrote that when correctly grown "it will become (of all other trees) the most proper and beautiful for walks, as producing an upright body, smooth and even bark, ample leaf, sweet blossom, the delight of bees, and a goodly shade at distance of eighteen or twenty-five foot. They are also very patient of pruning." That is still as correct as it was when in the great formal gardens of Europe it was the most widely used (and long-suffering) deciduous tree for every form of arboricultural ornament. He might have added that the stems are particularly flexible and can readily be trained, and that often in summer it is afflicted by aphides which deposit an unpleasant secretion.

Unfortunately, by far the usual lime in our avenues and ornamental plantings is still the common lime, *T. europaea* (or *vulgaris*). This is a hybrid of *T. cordata* and *T. platyphyllos* which still appears occasionally when the two grow together. It is very easily propagated by layering, which method was practised by the Dutch, as Evelyn records, from whom we imported great quantities, "to our excessive cost, while our own woods etc. in some places spontaneously produce them: and though of somewhat smaller leaf, yet altogether as good, apt to be civilized and made more florid. From thence I have received many of their berries: so as it is a shameful negligence, that we are not better provided of nurseries of a tree so choice and universally acceptable."

It is a disaster that Evelyn's advice was not accepted. All our old trees, and most younger ones, are disfigured by bushy growths—sometimes consisting of an immense number of twigs—which destroy the graceful appearance of the tree in winter, though in summer it is less noticeable, as they may be to some extent hidden by foliage. The unsightliness is not present on the large- and small-leaved limes (*T. platyphyllos* and *T. cordata*).

It has been suggested that this abnormal growth is a feature of the trees that have been raised vegetatively for centuries and that trees raised from seed* might not inherit it. Unfortunately, that is not so; incipient bushiness appears after a dozen or so years of age.

Avoid then, *T. europaea*.

T. cordata, the small-leaved lime, a British native particularly on calcareous formation, is a beautiful tree with markedly heart-shaped leaves and distinguished by flower spikes that spread rather than hang. It is a shapely, slow-growing tree, formerly grown in woodland for its coppice poles, which are very pliant. It is propagated from seed or layers.

T. euchlora is a large tree, with rich green leaves, of hybrid origin, introduced about a century ago. Free from aphid attack it showed great promise, but as trees mature they have developed most unsightly irregular growths in the crown. This tree should not be used. It must be propagated vegetatively.

T. petiolaris, the pendent silver lime, is a tall tree of great magnificence with a weeping habit. The large leaves are almost white underneath. It flowers freely after the other limes in late July and August. Unsuitable for training, it might well be more widely used for avenues, or, the inner branches removed, as a magnificent arbour. The fruit is infertile and the tree must be propagated vegetatively.

T. platyphyllos is a splendid tree of the largest size, now uncommon, which should over the centuries have been used for all the purposes that Evelyn indicated.

---

* There is a long-standing and entirely erroneous belief that seed from the European lime is infertile.

The leaves on some strains are not particularly large. It is easily raised from seed: the young plants grow vigorously. A red-twigged form, 'Rubra' ('Corallina') is probably more frequently planted than the type; this must be propagated by layering.

For those who enjoy the most distinctive scent of the limes, *T. platyphyllos* flowers first, *T. europaea* next, then *T. cordata* and finally *T. petiolaris*.

ULEX (*Leguminosae*)

The common gorse, *U. europaeus*, might well be used more as a wickedly spiny low hedge, particularly on light, heathy soils. The double form 'Plenus', with its fine, deep yellow flowers in early spring, might be considered. It is propagated from cuttings taken in August and kept close. When rooted, they should be potted-up and planted out the following winter—possibly ·5 m apart. The fastigiate or Irish gorse, *U. europaeus strictus*, does not flower freely.

ULMUS (*Ulmaceae*)

The elms have a long-established tradition as avenue and ornamental trees in our gardens and landscapes, but the risk of death from elm disease is always present. The small-growing extremely pendulous *Ulmus glabra* 'Camperdownii' is a possibility for an arbour. The commoner weeping wych elm, *U.g.* 'Pendula', is a much larger and wider-spreading tree, and only suitable for parks.

VIBURNUM (*Caprifoliaceae*)

The guelder rose (*V. opulus*) is found in hedgerows, usually on limestone or chalky foundations, growing to 4 m high. The white flowers open in early June. It is notable for its brilliant scarlet foliage as the leaves fade and its translucent red berries hanging on far into the winter. 'Notcutts Variety' has larger flowers and fruits than the type and "Xanthocarpum" very beautiful yellow berries. 'Sterile', the snowball tree, has large bosses of white flowers but, alas, no berries. The species come readily from seed and the variants from cuttings. Though unsuited for using as a hedge on their own, both the species and variants warrant planting in mixed hedges, particularly on alkaline soils.

V. lantana, the wayfaring tree, is also found in our hedges. It is deciduous and may reach the size of a small tree. The white flowers open in May and June, followed by black fruit. It is also a lime-lover, but has no particular attractions.

V. tinus, the laurustinus, is an evergreen native from the Mediterranean, which has been grown here for over three centuries, and has unfortunately been over-shadowed by subsequent introductions. What Loudon wrote about it cannot be bettered.

It "forms tufted truly evergreen shrubs, prolific in flowers; and in airy situations on dry soils, when they have room to attain large size, they become the most conspicuous ornaments of British gardens during winter and early spring. They do not thrive well in the smoke of cities; nevertheless they are to be seen nowhere finer than in the front gardens of small villas, from 5 to 20 miles from the metropolis; when they are in flower from November to April, and sometimes also in April, May and June. Its blossoms are white, and so abundant as to give a gay appearance to the plant even in midwinter, an effect which is greatly heightened by the lively shining green of the foliage, and by the varied and picturesque forms of the compact tufting of the branches. These plants are admirably adapted for forming flower garden hedges, and for varying the low iron palisades, pales or brick walls which separate the front gardens of street and suburban houses. The leaves, however, in these cases, should be removed as soon as they fall; as, when they dry, they have a remarkably fetid odour . . . All the varieties are readily propagated by cuttings, taken off in autumn, and planted in a sandy soil, on a northern border."

The flowers are pale rose-pink. 'Eve Price' has rather smaller leaves, with carmine buds and pink flowers. 'French White' has white flowers. 'Purpureum' has dark leaves and 'Variegatum' has leaves well variegated with gold, said not to be so hardy as the type.

CONIFERS

CEPHALOTAXUS (*Cephalolaxaceae*)

These large-leaved, yew-like, large shrubs or small trees of somewhat spreading growth might well be tried as hedges of an unusual kind in the milder districts. They will stand shade, drip and calcareous soils and can be clipped. They are recommended for this purpose in Dallimore and Jackson's *Handbook of Coniferae*, though I have never seen them so used. The largest is *C. fortunei*, the commonest *C. harringtonia drupacea* which has an erect growing cultivar 'Fastigiata', a sombre-foliaged small tree which can be seen growing at Wisley. Except for this last, wide spacing, say at 1·5 m, would seem desirable.

CHAMAECYPARIS (*Cupressaceae*)

The Lawson cypress with its many cultivated variants and cord-like shoots covered with small evergreen scale-like leaves is today the commonest conifer in gardens.

The type, *C. lawsoniana*, is quite often used in hedges or taller screens. For these purposes it is not ideal, by nature having a distinct narrow and pendulous top, being rather a sombre green, and the fact that a batch of seedlings almost invariably has plants of unevenly vigorous growth, thus taking a considerable time to fill out to make a level top. Nor is it of fast growth. (For this type of hedge, *Thuya plicata*, which see, is superior). It should be planted out in well worked but not richly manured ground when quite small (large plants tend to blow over) at about 1·5 m or rather closer.

For formal planting, the cultivar 'Allumii' is unexcelled as a narrowly pyramidal tree which needs no clipping. A newer introduction, 'Kilmacurragh', is a brighter green and the closest we can get to the narrow Italian cypress.

There are other forms which grow naturally to a shape that is equivalent to clipped trees. All are hardy, tolerant of all kinds of soils except those that are ill-drained, though they lose the freshness of their foliage in poor atmospheres.

CUPRESSOCYPARIS (*Cupressaceae*)

The Leyland cypress, *Cupressocyparis leylandii*, is a hybrid that arose towards the end of last century between the Nootka cypress (*Chamaecyparis nootkatensis*) and the Monterey cypress (*Cupressus macrocarpa*). It grows with immense vigour under almost all conditions, reaching 25–27 m. It is tolerant of seaside and urban air and will grow on chalk. Being easily propagated from cuttings (the seed is infertile), it has been widely used for screens and hedges. For the latter purpose wide planting—say 1 m or even more—is desirable. It has the disadvantage that the growth is so vigorous that when it has reached the required height it will need cutting twice or oftener a year, lastly in autumn.

CUPRESSUS (*Cupressaceae*)

The cypress of the classics (*C. sempervirens*) has already been discussed. Its tenderness, particularly when young, in exceptionally hard winters makes it unsatisfactory, except in mild districts. *C. macrocarpa*, growing naturally only in a small, windswept area by the sea around Monterey (hence its name Monterey cypress), withstands those conditions well and also grows on chalk. As it is easily raised from the abundant seed that it produces, it has been widely used for hedging. The small seedlings must be potted up and after a year's growth, when about 30 cm high, planted out about 60 cm apart. The young plants are subject to frost damage in the colder districts, but even worse is the fact that even in established hedges a severe winter will kill bushes here and there, quite destroying the appearance of the hedge. It should therefore only be used in the mildest localities.

JUNIPERUS (*Cupressaceae*)

Juniperus communis, a native, has already been mentioned. It is tolerant of all conditions, thriving on chalk. It is but little used today. Loudon wrote (1838): "The entire juniper bush was formerly employed in topiary work; and Evelyn mentions that his brother had an arbour, which three persons could sit in, cut out of a single plant. This arbour was 7 feet wide and 11 feet high. The juniper is occasionally still seen in modern gardens trained and clipped into the form of an open bowl or goblet. There is a fine specimen, a bowl, in the gardens of Mrs Marryatt, at Wimbledon House, and another in the nursery of Mr Waterer at Knaphill. In France, being one of the few evergreen shrubs that will stand the open air in the climate of Paris, it is often planted as a screen to objects which it is desired to conceal, and trained and clipped into the shape of evergreen walls called there *rideaux de verdure*."

Today it is little used for these purposes: I have never seen examples and have no experience of it. It is a slow-growing plant, not normally reaching any great height though a huge bush some 16 m high has been recorded. Naturally, it will grow in the most exposed places.

Two slow-growing erect varieties, *hibernica*, the Irish and *suecica*, the Swedish juniper are not really satisfactory, as they tend to fall apart after heavy snow, becoming shabby in age.

J. sabina, the savin, is a shrub of stiff habit and spreading growth usually found in nature on limestone. The leaves have a strong aromatic odour when bruised. It stands clipping well and was formerly used for low hedges, but is seldom seen now. It might be useful on poor, particularly chalky soils. It is easily raised from cuttings.

PICEA (*Pinaceae*)

It may seem odd to include the Norway spruce, *P. abies* or *excelsa* here. Yet it is seen in, for example, seventeenth-century Dutch garden pictures as a clipped tree. Loudon (1838) has this to say about it: "The tree bears the shears; and, as it is of rapid growth, it makes excellent hedges for shelter . . . At the Whim (an estate planted by the Duke of Argyll) a spruce fir hedge was planted, in 1823, with plants 10 feet high, put in 3 feet apart, and with the exception of three left to shoot up, for the purpose of being clipped into ornamental figures, the whole were cut down to 5 feet, and afterwards trimmed to an elaborate shape. The hedge was first cut on January 25th, the year after planting; and, as the plants were found to sustain no injury, about the end of that month has been chosen for cutting it every year since. Every portion of this hedge is beautiful and green; and the annual growths are very short, giving the surface of the hedge a fine healthy appearance."

As this spruce is produced in large quantities for forestry and is inexpensive, this suggests a much wider use for it in making screens and ornamental hedges.

PODOCARPUS (*Podocarpaceae*)

These attractive, yew-like shrubs and trees commonly called yellow woods are for the most part not hardy. Two species, however, are happy in all but the colder districts. *P. alpinus* resembles a miniature yew with cheerful, bright green leaves; it is slow growing and quite hardy, reaching about 60 cm. Planted about 30 cm apart, it might well be used as an original dwarf hedge. The plum-fruited yew, *P. andinus* (or *Prumnopitys elegans*), resembles a yew with almost glaucous foliage. It reaches tree size in mild districts, but in many other places could well be used as a hedge. Cuttings of side shoots can be rooted in a close frame during late summer and early autumn. They might be planted about 1 m apart.

TAXUS (*Taxaceae*)

Much has already been written about the yew on account of its hardiness, long life, ability to suffer the most drastic cutting and adaptability to all types of soils except those that are not well drained. In reiterating something of what has been said previously to bring it into line with the other subjects in this section, one must first emphasize that given good conditions yew is not slow growing. The ground must therefore be well prepared in advance by digging a strip where the hedge or plant is to grow at least 1 m wide and working in plenty of dung (if available) or otherwise compost and bonemeal. This should be done well before the planting is to take place. The actual hedge illustrated, facing page 97, was planted under such conditions and consisted of bushy plants about 60 cm high put in about the same distance apart. They were plants obtained from a nurseryman and were good quality with bushy roots. A wattle fence was used to protect them, as the site was windy— but this, though a help, is not essential. Planting was done in autumn. The young hedge was regularly mulched with lawn mowings. The sides were regularly cut back quite hard, so that the base was wider than the top. It is important not to cut the leading shoots at the top until the required height is reached. In this case it was 1·5 m just five years after planting. A year or two afterwards the hedge was evenly dense throughout.

Pruning is best done in early summer. In the case of very old, overgrown specimens it may be very severe; in such cases it is advisable to carry out the work in stages.

Propagation is from the abundantly produced seed which germinates the second spring after sowing. Cuttings of variants which do not come true from seed root easily when taken in late summer. Old hedges benefit greatly from a dressing of fertilizer or compost.

Yew is not ideal where atmospheric pollution is bad, for, though it will survive, the foliage loses its sheen. Nor does it like exposed seaside conditions.

Cultivation of specimens for topiary is on the same lines, remembering never to cut back the leading shoots of parts whose further growth is needed.

Today when the cultivation of flowers takes pride of place in most gardens, particularly those flowering early in the year when there is little green leafage the yew hedge is paramount as a hedge to enhance their display while still, of course, retaining its feature as the most important live, evergreen architectonic element in garden design.

While yew hedges are scarcely the most suitable hosts for climbing plants it is worth mentioning that the most elegant and fiery red *Tropaeolum speciosum* can, in those local circumstances in which it will thrive, be established on the shady side of a yew hedge with great effect.

Of variants of the yew suitable for hedging, the golden yew, 'Elegantissima', is a fine colour.

There are several variants which, even without clipping, take their place in the formal garden. Most frequently seen is the Irish yew, 'Fastigiata', very erect and slim in youth, but becoming rather pot-bellied in old age; the golden form of this, 'Fastigiata Aurea', is good. Their use has already been mentioned.

THUYA (*Cupressaceae*)

The thuyas or arbor-vitae are evergreen trees some of which are of considerable value in the garden.

T. occidentalis, the American arbor-vitae, was probably the first North American tree to be grown in Europe. It was being grown in England in 1597. It is today particularly associated with Victorian church-yard planting, being of slow, rather erect growth and needing no maintenance whatever. The leaves turn a rather drab bronze colour in winter. It was, Loudon wrote in 1838, widely used to form hedges and shelters—a purpose for which on account of its hardiness and prolific production of seed it might well be used today. It has a variant, "Fastigiata", which is an excellent slow-growing narrowly columnar tree, referred to earlier.

T. plicata is in every way a contrast to the foregoing. Known to and increasingly grown in our forests under the misleading name of western red cedar, where it reaches a large size, experience has shown that it stands clipping well and makes a fine hedge, retaining the rich, glossy green of its fragrant leaves on fern-like shoots throughout the year. Further, it can be trained up to make a hedge of a considerable height, while left unpruned it will make a surprisingly even-growing and dense screen. A particularly narrow form is 'Fastigiata'. A lovely variant that grows vigorously is 'Zebrina', which has leaves striped with bright yellow—though whether this is available in quantity for what would be a most decorative hedge I do not know. The type is best obtained from forest tree nurserymen who raise it extensively, though it is rather more expensive than other forest trees owing to a disease that affects the small seedlings. For hedging, it should be treated more or less the same as yew.

TSUGA (*Pinaceae*)

The hemlock spruces are mostly large trees unsuitable for hedges. However, *T. heterophylla* now increasingly planted in our forests (where it will bear dense shade and is of vigorous growth) has been planted apparently with every success as a hedge experimentally in, among other places, Edinburgh Botanic Gardens. The leaves are narrow and not very spruce-like. It will not grow on shallow chalk soils.

APPENDIX II

Some Books

Amherst, the Hon. A., *A history of gardening in England*. 1896.

Anderson, James, *The new practical gardener*. 1871.

Bacon, F., *Of gardens*. 1625.

Bagot, A., *Levens Hall*. n.d.

Bean, W. J., *Trees and shrubs hardy in the British Isles*. 1929–36.

Blomfield, R., *The formal garden in England*. 1892 (1901 ed.).

Cook, M., *The manner of raising, ordering and improving forest trees*. 1676 and 1717.

Dallimore, W., *Holly, yew and box*. 1908.

Dallimore, W., and Jackson, A. B., *A handbook of coniferae*. 1948.

Elwes, H. J., and Henry, A., *Trees of Great Britain and Ireland*. 1906–13.

Evelyn, J., *Sylva or a discourse on forest trees*. 1664, etc.

Fiennes, C., *The Journeys of Celia Fiennes*, ed. Morris, C., 1947.

Gilpin, W., *Remarks on forest scenery and other woodland views*. 1791.

Gilpin, W. S., *Practical hints upon landscape gardening*. 1832.

Godwin, H., *A history of the British flora*. 1956.

Green, D., *Gardener to Queen Anne*. 1956.

Haddington, the Earl of, *A short treatise on forest trees*. 1765.
    Forest trees, ed. Anderson, M. L., 1953.

Hadfield, M., *British trees*. 1957.
    Landscape with trees. 1967.
    A history of British gardening. 1969.

Hanmer, Sir, T., *The garden book of* . . . (1659), ed. Elstob, I., 1933.

Henry, A., see Elwes, H. J., and Henry, A.

Hillier and Sons, *Catalogue of trees and shrubs*. 1964.

Hunt, P. (editor), *The Shell gardens book*. 1964.

Hussey, C., *English gardens and landscapes 1700–1750*. 1967.

James, J., *The theory and practice of gardening*. 1712.

Jekyll, G., *Garden ornament*. 1918.

Kent, A. H., *A manual of the Coniferae.* 1881.
    Veitch's manual of the Coniferae. 1900.
Lawson, W., *A new orchard and garden.* 1631 (reprint of 1927).
Lloyd, N., *Garden craftsmanship in yew and box.* 1925.
Loudon, J. C., *Arboretum et fruticetum Brittanicum.* 1838.
    An encyclopaedia of gardening. 1827.
Lowe, J., *Yew trees of Great Britain and Ireland.* 1897.
Miller, P., *The gardener's dictionary.* 1748 ed.
Parkinson, J., *Paradisi in sole paradisus terrestris.* 1629.
Price, Sir U., *An essay on the picturesque.* 1796.
    Essays on the picturesque. 1798.
Ray, J., *Historia plantarum.* 1686.
Robinson, W., *The English flower garden.* 1896 ed.
Sedding, J. D., *Garden craft old and new.* 1890.
Sieveking, A. F., *The praise of gardens.* 1899.
Sitwell, Sir G., *An essay on the making of gardens.* 1909.
Tipping, H. A., *English gardens.* 1925.
Veitch, J., and Sons, see Kent, A. H.

Note: Quotations from literary sources are taken from standard editions.

Olearia macrodonta 'Major'
in June (page 79)

Prunus laurocerasus 'Zabelliana'
in mid-May (page 81)

A newly planted yew hedge (page 92)

Severe pruning
of an over-grown
yew hedge (page 92)

Index